Praise for The Will to Be

"This excellent book shows you that your willingness to be and do whatever it takes is the key to lifelong happiness."
—Brian Tracy, author of *The Power of Self-Confidence*

"William Lindsey's new book is packed with valuable information. I read it and came away greatly uplifted and encouraged."
Pat Williams, author of *The Mission Is Remission*, Orlando Magic Senior Vice President

"The inspiring ideas Pastor Lindsey shares in *The Will to Be* are dynamic and life-changing! Read this book from cover to cover, put his principles into practice, and begin to see a positive breakthrough in your life!"
—Ryan C. Lowe, author of *Get Off Your Attitude*

"*The Will to Be* is for people who want to change their current state of life. The book will assist you in thinking the correct way . . . which is God's way. Once you change your thinking, you change your future. How do you want your future?"
—Paul "Showtime" Gaffney, Harlem Globetrotter, CEO and Founder, Chattanooga Rail Runners

"In his new book, *The Will to Be: Becoming More Than What You Are*, William J. Lindsey sketches a distinctive path for accomplishing personal aspirations. The breadth and scope of this book will surely stimulate your thinking and launch you into flight on a course to reach ing your destiny, your f ll potential, and living out your true owe it to yourself to read this book

T0142532

his career in ministry, Lindsey once again helps us think clearly about relevant life issues. He recommends that readers prepare to experience a transformation of the mind. This is true . . . and much, much more."

—Pamela Breaux, English Language Arts Instructional Officer, Doctoral Candidate at Nova Southeastern University

"There is no better time in our world than now for a book that encourages people to live fearlessly and fully in God's promises. This phenomenal book, *The Will to Be*, is a clear reminder of the power that awaits us when we seize the moment and take charge of our lives. William J. Lindsey offers valuable, practical methods for doing so."

—Rudy Rasmus, author of *Touch: Pressing Against the Wounds of a Broken World*, Pastor of St. John's UMC-Houston, TX, On-Air personality, SiriusXM

"The insights revealed in this book are compelling truths that lead people to move from what is to what ought to be. Readers will be challenged to believe in their God-given purpose and abilities and to become the person they were destined to be. I recommend it to anyone seeking to go above and beyond the status quo."

—Dr. John D. Ogletree Jr., Pastor of First Metropolitan Church, Houston, Texas

"*The Will to Be* is a must-read for everyone! After reading this masterful work of literary art, I guarantee you that you will *never* entertain failure as an option. I encourage you to take these divinely inspired principles and apply them to your daily living. Thank you, William J. Lindsey, for pursuing your purpose by penning such a life-changing manifesto! I highly endorse every word."

—Jonita Reynolds, EdD
Chief Executive Officer, Gulf Coast Community Services
Association, Inc.

"The lion is not the strongest animal in the jungle, neither is it the largest, fastest, or most intelligent animal of them all; however, the lion is known as the king of the jungle because of its 'will' power. This comprehensive book by William J. Lindsey, *The Will to Be,* is a catalyst that will awaken the sleeping lion in you; it will awaken your inner greatness and challenge your perception of your true potential. If you looking to be more than you ever thought possible. I recommend you engage with this book packed with gems of wisdom that will unlock your 'will to be.'"

—Phinehas Kinuthia, Senior Pastor, Global Enlightenment
Center and author of *Dreaming to Becoming*

"*The Will to Be* is an inspiring back-pocket guide to what God's true 'will' for believers can become. William J. Lindsey cleverly and chronically explains . . . if you have the faith, will, and obedience to God, then you certainly can experience a wonderful life."

—Frederick Walker, EdD

"This book is for right now, on decisions to help you face your everyday spiritual and personal growth. In this book, William J. Lindsey has many great quotes to push your 'will to be' when life tries to slow you down. I highly recommend this book!"

—SGM Steven R. Johnson, U.S. Army Reserve

"*The Will to Be* is an incredible read that truly enriches your spiritual growth! Profoundly thought provoking, you will be challenged to your inner core. From start to finish, this insightful read equips you with the necessary spiritual tools to garner the willpower to rise above your adversity in order to claim God's blessings for your life! William J. Lindsey's principles in *The Will to Be* are practical and easily applicable to your spiritual and professional life! It has helped me to better understand God's powerful purpose for my life and will do the same for you!"

—Amy Benya, Esq., Civil Attorney

"I highly recommend this book to everyone. We all need words of encouragement from time to time. Author William Lindsey has very special and unique skills to inspire and provoke thought with his words. I literally could not put this book down, and I normally don't read books that are not about sports or electronics. This book will truly inspire everyone to achieve their goals in life and recover from life's many setbacks. A great read, you cannot wait for the next chapter."

—Sgt. Russell Dukes Jr., Houston Police Department

"*The Will to Be* contains vital, practical and relevant tools . . . to be your best and to live the best life that God intended. Whether you are strong-willed, have high expectations, or need encouragement, *The Will to Be* will certainly help and encourage you as you walk through life.

—Denise R. Eaton, Adjunct Faculty, SHSU

"William J. Lindsey's compassion and commitment with this gifted book truly shows his heart-felt, down-to-earth desire to share his beliefs and everyday living. I'm so inspired by the way he tells it like it is and reminds us what's expected for our life. If life has always challenged you, this book is truly the key to unlock where you are stuck. He dramatically illustrates our possibilities on point. I look forward to changing the chapters in my life. *The Will to Be* has encouraged me tremendously. I recommend this awesome read to everyone who wishes to live with joy, peace, purpose, and abundance."

—Millicent, Brooklyn, New York

"If you desire a fired-up soul full of energy, drive, and motivation to fulfill your God-given potential, *The Will to Be* is a must-read. William J. Lindsey's *The Will to Be* awakens the oftentimes forgotten and dormant ingredient of our soul—the will. Jam-packed with insightful, mind-grabbing, and practical truths, *The Will to Be* will stimulate uncharted thoughts and set ablaze untapped possibilities. Thank you, William, for the rekindling of my soul!"

—Dr. Troy Williams Sr., Lead Pastor, The Mosaic Church: Discipleship Is Membership; Executive Pastor, The Redemption House

After reading "The Will To Be", I realized that I can't change or control the natural disasters in my life, but I can control my attitude and my will to succeed. William J. Lindsey has written a wonderful book for those who are tired of surviving and striving, and are ready to thrive. If you are at a crossroad in life, pick a copy of "The Will To Be" to be your compass.

Uche O'Brien, Nigeria

"This book will transform how you view your true purpose for living every day. It will give you the fuel to do the things you were designed to do. Be prepared to undergo a metamorphosis and become the best version of you—the you God created you to be."

"*The Will to Be* is an attention-captivating, mind-set-changing book. It inspires you to evaluate where you are in life then equips you with the tools and motivation needed to really *live* to your full capacity. It is definitely more than any other book on your shelf; it is an asset for life.

"This inspiring book, *The Will to Be*, is packed with relevant, life-changing ideals that will both motivate and challenge you to be all that God has called you to be.

"This book will enhance your quality of life and help expand your level of thinking and your faith to realize that you are designed by God for a purpose. This book will help you desire and seek the purpose that God has designed you for. It will give you the 'will' to live on purpose for God. I love this book! It is a great read and I recommend that everyone read this book and begin to live your life on purpose!"

the will to be

BECOMING MORE THAN WHAT YOU ARE

William J. Lindsey

WESTBOW°
PRESS
A DIVISION OF THOMAS NELSON
& ZONDERVAN

Unless otherwise noted, all Scripture quotations are taken from the New King James Version®. Copyright © 1982 by Thomas Nelson, Inc. Used by permission. All rights reserved.

Scripture quotations marked KJV are taken from the King James Version of the Bible (Public Domain).

Scripture quotations marked NIV are taken from the Holy Bible, New International Version®. NIV®. Copyright © 1973, 2011 by Biblica, Inc.™ Used by permission of Zondervan. All rights reserved worldwide. www.zondervan.com.

Scripture quotations marked NLT are taken from the Holy Bible, New Living Translation, copyright © 1996, 2007 by Tyndale House Foundation. Used by permission of Tyndale House Publishers, Inc., Carol Stream, Illinois 60188.

WestBow Press books may be ordered through booksellers or by contacting:

WestBow Press
A Division of Thomas Nelson & Zondervan
1663 Liberty Drive
Bloomington, IN 47403
www.westbowpress.com
1 (866) 928-1240

ISBN: 978-1-4908-4522-7 (sc)
ISBN: 978-1-4908-4523-4 (hc)
ISBN: 978-1-4908-4521-0 (e)

Library of Congress Control Number: 2014914383

Printed in the United States of America.

WestBow Press rev. date: 09/26/2014

Dedicated to my mom, the late great Jewel Delores Lindsey. Thank you for your life, love, laughter, leadership, and legacy. You are my rock, the wind beneath my wings. You are a precious jewel, a fine gem. I will never let your legacy die; your descendants will know you and call you blessed. You will always be my heroine and I will always be your biggest fan. Thank for your resilient leadership, your amazing faith, and your constant love.

You taught me how to have "the will to be."

Acknowledgments

I want to thank God for giving me a desire to put my thoughts on paper and to help me launch my first book, *The Will to Be,* for without Him I could have done none of this. I also want to acknowledge my amazing wife and best friend, Shawn Lindsey, for her loyalty and support. She helps me go above and beyond. To my two amazing adult kids, whom I love relentlessly, thanks for giving Dad some space to write and believing in my dream to authorship. To the many generous endorsers who kindly put their interpretation on *The Will to Be,* thank you very much. To the many friends and family who supported, prayed, and kept cheering me on until I cross the finish line, from the bottom of my heart, much obliged!

Contents

When I want to read a good book, I write one.
Benjamin Disraeli

Introduction

Life is a process of becoming, a combination of states we have to go through. Where people fail is that they wish to elect a state and remain in it. This is a kind of death.

—Anais Nin

Today is the first day of the *best* of your life. All you really have is *today*. Tomorrow is not promised to any of us. Yesterday is history, but *today* is a great day to become more than what you are. *Today* is a great day to be better than you were yesterday. *Today* is a great day to become fully alive. *Today* is the day the Lord has made. *Today* is a great day to become God's best version of you. *Today* you must be intentional and predetermined to make your life count. TODAY.

Twenty-four hours make a day, 168 hours make a week, 52 weeks make a year, and a few more years make one life. In other words, life is too short to live on accident.

Many people are living life randomly, by chance. Many people have lost their will to become more than what they could be—maybe because of pain, people, or problems they have experienced. When you lose your will, you lose your way. The power of your will is the power of choice and the deliberate action or intention resulting from the exercise of this power.

Abraham Maslow said, "If you deliberately set out to be less than you are capable, you'll be unhappy for the rest of your life." Too many unhappy people are walking around, faking the funk. If they would just exercise the willpower God has given them, they could move toward a more fulfilling life. With your will, you can expect, anticipate, dream, envision, hope, and look forward to a better you and a better tomorrow.

The Will to Be reaffirms the invincibility of the human spirit. It's a book not meant to be read only, but a book to be experienced, explored, and applied. This book is not just a recommended read, it's a required read for those who are trying to live out their passion and become more than they are. The power of your will is one of the most powerful gifts you possess. You must have the will and be willing to become an improved version of you. I believe you can develop and evolve into the work of art that God created you to be. There's more to you than meets the eye: far more potential, much more definition, and significantly more capacity.

Applying the principles in this book will help you transform your mind-set and allow a metamorphosis to take place in your life and spirit. You will not only become a better you, you will make progress toward becoming your best version of you, the very you that God created you to become. So expect a major shift in your thinking, because if you change your thinking, you can change your life. The wisest man ever to live told us, "As he [a person] thinks in his heart, so is he" (Prov. 23:7).

The Will To Be

So prepare to allow what you experience in this book to guide you to reshape your thinking and reform your mind. This manifesto is pregnant with insight and inspiration, so grab your pen, pencil, and highlighter, and prepare to break loose and escape mediocrity, apathy, and normality and embrace a mind-expanding experience. In the words of B. C. Forbes, "It may be alright to be content with what you have; never with what you are."

Thank you for your willingness to become more than you are, and may you never, ever stop arriving.

1

The Will to Be

The greatest of all miracles is that we need not be tomorrow what we are today, but we can improve if we make use of the potential implanted in us by God.

—Rabbi Samuel M. Silver

In Lewis Carroll's classic *Alice in Wonderland*, Alice comes to the junction in the road that leads in different directions. She asks the Cheshire Cat for advice:

"CheshirePuss . . . would you tell me, please, which way I ought to go from here?"

"That depends a good deal on where you want to get to," said the Cat.

"I don't much care where," said Alice.

"Then it doesn't matter which way you go," said the Cat.

That's so true. If you don't care about where you're going in life, it doesn't matter which road you take. But if you are like many people, you are living life as it comes, and you don't know which way to go. You are indecisive, pointless, and without aim. I believe you are headed either somewhere or nowhere.

In her life-planning book, *Me: Five Years from Now*, author Sheree Bykofsky asked a very important question: "You wouldn't go traveling to an unknown place without a map or directions of some sort, so why do that in life?"

I've met many good and gifted people who have lost their will, their drive, and their tenacity to become more than what they are. Many people are coasting through life, living life in cruise control. Instead of taking the road best traveled, they prefer to ease on down the road of least resistance. They have allowed challenges, setbacks, or a lack of discipline to keep them locked in a mental and spiritual prison. Many people are stuck in the quicksand of mediocrity because of the paralysis of analysis. I don't believe we should survive and strive; I believe God wants us to thrive.

With heaven backing us, we can will ourselves out of poverty, complacency, debt, addictions, illiteracy, and other bad habits that constantly defeat us.

If you can will your way out of backward living, you can will your way into forward living. I'm not saying life is easy; in the words of M. Scott Peck in his classic *The Road Less Traveled*, "life is difficult."

Maybe you've encountered several painful things that were beyond your control: You can't control who your parents were, you can't control where you were born or your skin complexion. You can't control whether you were born into poverty or riches. But one thing you can control, and that is your attitude and your will to succeed. With the power of faith you can leap out of the quicksand of complacency and reach for new levels of living. God is still in control, and we should always include Him in the equation of our life plans. It reminds me of the old song we used to sing in the Baptist church that my dad once pastored across from the railroad track: "Without God I could do nothing, without Him I would fail, without Him my life would be rugged like a ship without a sail."

Remember, God has given each of us a will to deliberately decide upon a course of action. I don't believe it's all on God. God holds us responsible to do our part. Ben Franklin was right when he said, "God helps those who help themselves." Many people use the statement "I'm just waiting on God" as a crutch not to do anything with their lives, when in reality God is waiting on them.

In national best seller *The Gospel of Good Success*, Kirbyjon H. Caldwell, who pastors the Windsor Village United Methodist Church in Houston, Texas, wrote:

> Why have you been "spared"? It's up to you to determine the reason and live out God's primary purpose and promise for your life. God's promises of success are incomplete, however, without your faithful response. God may promise, but you must push. God may declare, but you must decide to pursue that Divine declaration. God may will it, but you must walk it out. In other words, God's supernatural power is maximized when it is coupled with your faithful application of your God-given ability. Remember this equation: God's supernatural ability plus your faithfulness to act equals success.[1]

We must be intentional about becoming more than we are. We must use our time wisely. We are rigorously limited to seven days a week, which means we have 168 hours a week or 10,080 minutes a week. We must make our time count and understand that time is a gift from God.

In the mid-1970s, I was walking home from Bethune elementary school one day. This guy drove by in his low rider, with the speaker volume turned up high. I heard the lyrics "Time keeps on slipping, slipping, slipping into the future." Those words were more powerful than the heavy beat of that song. They stuck to me like Velcro, because it was sort of a revelation of how time keeps moving into the future. Benjamin Franklin said, "Lost time is never found again." You can lose your career and get another; you can lose your home and get another; you can lose your car and get another; you can lose your money and earn more; but if you lose time, you will never get it back again.

Each of us lives minute by minute. It doesn't matter how old we are, where we live, or how much money we have, we're each allotted 1,440 minutes per day. We can decide to waste our minutes or harness them to our advantage to build a better life. We can sleep them away or squeeze every opportunity from them.

What will you do with your minutes?

We must have a yearning, burning desire to use our minutes wisely and to reach our maximum potential. As you engage this book, I suggest you approach it with a winning, optimistic attitude and a willingness to apply these simple but profound principles. Sure, it will require discipline to live them out. But if you do, you will become much more productive in your life. In the words of Zig Ziglar, "You are the only person on earth who can use your ability."

Life is like a ten-speed bike, and most people are stuck in first gear because they have never shifted into a higher gear. It's time to make a shift, change gears, and double-clutch to your next level of spiritual and personal growth. Desire to be more. Play offense with your life and take advantage of the opportunities before you.

Your life is meant for you to show up, step up, play your role, make your mark, and reach the zenith of your purpose in life. You have an appointment with purpose and a date with destiny. In simple terms, life is meant to be lived. These sayings about life are attributed to Mother Teresa:

> *Life is an opportunity, benefit from it.*
> *Life is beauty, admire it.*
> *Life is a dream, realize it.*
> *Life is a challenge, meet it.*
> *Life is a duty, complete it.*
> *Life is a game, play it.*
> *Life is a promise, fulfill it.*
> *Life is sorrow, overcome it.*
> *Life is a song, sing it.*
> *Life is a struggle, accept it.*
> *Life is a tragedy, confront it.*
> *Life is an adventure, dare it.*
> *Life is luck, make it.*
> *Life is too precious, do not destroy it.*
> *Life is life, fight for it.*

What a powerful yet true definition of life. I beg you to live your life to the fullest, to the max, until your life overflows. Robert Byrne said, "The purpose of life is a life of purpose." You have a reason to get out of bed and off the couch. It's called purpose; it's called destiny; it's called predetermination; it's called predestination. Your life is neither an accident nor a mistake. You're meant to live out your life completely, to show up on the platform of life and deliver a stellar performance. I love what Erma Bombeck said about life: "When I stand before God at the end of my life, I would hope that I would not have a single bit of talent left, and could say, 'I used everything you gave me.'" I encourage you to use everything you have, every bit, every piece, every crumb, every possible dot that you have. Former legendary Green Bay Packers coach Vince Lombardi said, "The spirit, the will to win, and the will to excel are the things that endure. These qualities are so much more important than the events that occur."

Regardless of the cards life has dealt you, if you hold God's hand, you make the rest of your life the best of your life.

Don't worry about the time you've lost; you can't change that. Refocus on the time you have left. Pray a Moses prayer, "Teach us to number our days, that we may gain a heart of wisdom" (Ps. 90:12).

Trust me, you can and should do this. Create a sense of urgency and take responsibility for your life. You don't want to reach the end of your life and look back with regret for the missed opportunities. Yes, it costs to become more than what you are, but in the words of Ruben Gonzalez, "The price of success weighs ounces. The price of regret weighs tons." Trust me, you don't want to look back with a shouldn't, couldn't, wouldn't attitude.

The moment you picked up this book and started to read it, a destiny moment was birthed in your life, and a new chapter of opportunities began. This book can be the commencement you've been waiting for, a book that can help you leave the comforts of the shore so you can explore the oceans of possibilities and opportunities. This book can help take you from shallow thinking and launch you into the deeper levels of possibility thinking; it can help you to leave mediocrity and embrace a life that's above and beyond ordinary. You must want it, will it, and be willing to work it.

Takeaway Points

We must have a yearning, burning desire to use our minutes wisely and to reach our maximum potential.

You have an appointment with purpose and a date with destiny.

You're meant to live out your life completely, show up on the platform of life, and deliver a stellar performance.

Don't worry about the time you've lost; you can't change that. Refocus on the time you have left.

Questions to Reflect On

What steps will you take to become more than what you are?

How has your understanding of the power of your will been enlightened?

What were some of the behaviors that have kept you limited in the past?

What is your biggest obstacle to becoming more than you are?

2

The Will to Dream

What happens to a dream deferred?
Does it dry up like a raisin in the sun?
Or fester like a sore—And then run?
Does it stink like rotten meat?
Or crust and sugar over—like a syrupy sweet?
Maybe it just sags like a heavy load.
Or does it explode?

"A Dream Deferred," Langston Hughes

Many people have been birthed with dreams: the dream of becoming an athlete, the dream of becoming a doctor, the dream of becoming the president of a university, or the dream of becoming an attorney. Many dream of becoming a singer, rapper, or artist. No matter what your dream is, it can come to pass. What many discover on the road to dreams-come-true is a season of delayed dreams. Between dream and destiny is the process of learning, growing, and maturing.

6-Step Process of the Dream Process

1. Desire
2. Decision
3. Discipline
4. Determination
5. Dependence on God
6. Destiny

4-Step Process of the Dream Test

1. Delays
2. Detours
3. Difficulties
4. Dream Busters

When your dream is deferred, don't stop dreaming—redream. Your dream will be tested to see if it's really a dream. Don't stop dreaming because of a delay; instead, dream even bigger. I love the story of Joseph in the Bible.

Joseph was the eleventh of Jacob's twelve sons and Rachel's firstborn. His half-brothers hated him because he was favored by his father but more so for his dreams.

Joseph, "the dreamer," once told his brothers about a dream that a day would come when they would all bow down to him. This dream made his brothers angrier. One day they saw Joseph in the distance. "Here comes that dreamer!" they said to one another.

Because of their jealousy and hatred, they plotted to kill him. But one of the brothers thought that was going too far, so they decided to sell Joseph into slavery. (See Genesis 37:18–28.)

His own brothers mocked him, ridiculed him, and laughed at him all because of his dreams. Big dreams invite haters into your life. If you ever want some haters, just start dreaming.

Big dreams cost something: hard work, money, sacrifice, energy, burning midnight oil.

Rick Warren once said, "You cannot put a small price tag on big dreams."

When you share your dream with other people, be prepared for them to laugh at you. Ira Flatow, in his book *They All Laughed . . . From Light Bulbs to Lasers*, shares numerous stories of people who were laughed at because of their dreams. Yet these dreams became reality and forever changed our lives. People laughed at Thomas Edison and called him crazy when he talked about his dream of creating a bulb of light that was not a candle. They laughed at Alexander Graham Bell and called him called him crazy when he talked about a machine you could talk through to other people in other places. They laughed at Christopher Columbus and called him crazy when he said the world was not flat, but round—and he was willing to fall off the edge to prove it. They laughed at the Wright Brothers and called them crazy when they said they would create a flying machine. They laughed at Martin Luther King Jr. and called him crazy when he talked about nonviolent civil rights demonstrations; and when he said he wanted to have a rally on the steps of the Lincoln Memorial to share his dreams with the world, they laughed harder. They laughed at John F. Kennedy when he said men would reach the moon before the end of the 1960s.[1] The list goes on and on. Most people laughed at these dreamers! They may laugh at you and your dreams, but don't be discouraged, because you will be among an elite group who outlasted their critics.

In 1993, while working in a hot warehouse, my coworkers laughed at me when I told them I was going to start a church with nobody, no building, no money, and no backing. People laugh at great dreams and great dreamers. The greater your dreams, the more people will laugh.

If you want to be talked about, have no dreams; but if you want to be laughed at, have big dreams.

You're either dreaming or dying. When you dream, you are expanding your horizon, enlarging your thinking, and advancing your future. Harriet Tubman said, "Every great dream begins with a dreamer. Always remember, you have within you the strength, the patience, and the passion to reach for the stars to change the world."

Your dream will keep you up some nights and wake you up on other nights. Do more than possess your dream; your dream must possess you. Do not let a lack of finances stop you from dreaming. Do not let a lack of support stop you from dreaming. Do not let naysayers stop you from dreaming. Your dream is priceless, and your dream should excite you. Your dream should cause your heart to pump and give you an adrenaline rush, because you know that it will make a noticeable difference in the world.

In his inspiring book on fulfilling dreams, *From Dreaming to Becoming*, international speaker and author Phinehas Kinuthia wrote, "A dream is a dominant idea that is ever present within us and constantly provokes us to greatness and awakens a desire to want to do all that we can to be more than we are. A dream is not idle thoughts; nor is it temporary fascinations or infatuations. A dream is God's blueprint regarding your potential future. It is meant to inspire hope and birth expectation, which motivates action toward what could be rather than what is."[2]

Howard Thurman was right when he pronounced, "A dream is the bearer of a new possibility, the enlarged horizon, the great hope."

A dream is a series of pictures in motion. Picture yourself living your dream.

1. You Must Visualize It
2. You Must Vocalize It
3. You Must Actualize It

That's what Martin Luther King did in 1963 on the March to Washington, one of the largest political rallies for human rights in United States history. Standing in front of the Lincoln Memorial, King delivered his historic "I Have a Dream" speech advocating racial harmony. "I have a dream that one day this nation will rise up and live out the true meaning of its creed: 'We hold these truths to be self-evident, that all men are created equal.'" Today we are living out Dr. King's dream, and, although someone killed the dreamer, the dream continues.

We grow and mature through our dreams. Dreams work if we are willing to work them. If you stopped dreaming your dream that you should have implemented long ago, I highly recommend that you pick up that dream, dust it off, speak some new life into it, and dream again—redream.

Remember the words of Eleanor Roosevelt: "The future belongs to those who believe in the beauty of their dreams." Believe in your dreams and be willing to make the necessary sacrifices to see them come true. Your dream is a solution to a problem. Walt Disney said, "All our dreams can come true, if we have the courage to pursue them."

It's not too late and you're not too old to fulfill your dreams. George Edward Foreman ("Big George") is a retired American professional boxer, former two-time World Heavyweight Champion, Olympic gold medalist, ordained Baptist minister, author, and entrepreneur. After dropping out of school at age fifteen, he trained in California as a boxer for a couple of years. Then he went on to be a gold medalist at the 1968 Olympics. Foreman won the World Heavyweight title in 1973 with a second round knockout of then-undefeated Joe Frazier in Kingston, Jamaica. He made two successful title defenses before losing to Muhammad Ali in The Rumble in the Jungle in 1974. He fought on but was unable to secure another title and retired following a loss to Jimmy Young in 1977. He became a Christian minister. But the dream to become the heavyweight champion of the world never left his soul. Ten years after retiring, Foreman announced a comeback, and in November 1994, at age forty-five, he regained the Heavyweight Championship by knocking out Michael Moorer. He remains the oldest Heavyweight Champion in history. He retired in 1997 at the age of forty-eight, with a final record of 76–5, including sixty-eight knockouts.

What if George had said, "I'm too old," "I'm too slow," or "I've wasted too much time"? George would not have made history.

I like to define *history* as His-story. God has a story for each of us to tell. What is your story telling others about dreams, endurance, and perseverance?

George's story keeps getting better. As one of the world's most beloved athletes and personalities, George is an ordained minister and the author of ten books. He has made millions from infomercials marketing the George Foreman Lean Mean Grilling Machine, which has sold more than 100 million units. He has also launched a number of successful products and services. His list of successes continues to grow because George continues to dream. In his book *Knockout Entrepreneur*, George wrote this about dreaming: "When one dream dies or comes to an end, don't wallow in despair. Dream a new dream and then work hard to see it come to pass." I encourage you not to give up on your dream.

The poem "Don't Quit" is reassurance that our dreams can come true.

When things go wrong, as they sometimes will,
When the road you're trudging seems all uphill,
When the funds are low and the debts are high,
And you want to smile, but you have to sigh,
When care is pressing you down a bit—
Rest if you must, but don't you quit.

Life is queer with its twists and turns,
As every one of us sometimes learns,
And many a fellow turns about
When he might have won had he stuck it out.
Don't give up though the pace seems slow—
You may succeed with another blow.

Often the goal is nearer than,
It seems to a faint and faltering man;
Often the struggler has given up
When he might have captured the victor's cup;
And he learned too late when the night slipped down,
How close he was to the golden crown.
Success is failure turned inside out—
The silver tint in the clouds of doubt,
And you never can tell how close you are,
It may be near when it seems afar;
So stick to the fight when you're hardest hit—
It's when things seem worst that you must not quit.

—*Edgar A. Guest*

Never quit on your dreams, and keep your will to see them come to pass. Most people quit on their dreams because they feel like they are too old. Truth be told, age is nothing but a number. Countless people did their best work in their later years. Colonel Sanders founded Kentucky Fried Chicken at age sixty-five; Winston Churchill became Prime Minister of Britain at age sixty-five; Moses was eighty years old when he led the children of Israel out of Egypt; and Abraham was an old man before he became the father of many nations. Zig Ziglar was right when he said, "The basic problem is that many people are afraid of their own dreams." Embrace your dream, engage your dream, and implement your dream. It's not too late; you're not too old.

You must do more than possess your dream; your dream must possess you.

The reason you're still reading this book proves that it's not too late for you to live out your dream. Langston Hughes said it best: "Hold fast to dreams, for if dreams die, life is a broken-winged bird that cannot fly."

When a bird breaks its wing, it is immobilized, unable to fly or possibly even to move around. It certainly cannot soar to greater heights. A broken-winged bird will never be able to reach its fullest potential. Birds were created to fly—and both wings are necessary. When your dreams fall apart, part of you dies and evaporates. Part of you expires and fades away. Don't give up on your dreams. Big dreams will be tested and tried. So never give up, no matter who leaves you, abandons you, or betrays you. No matter how long it takes, hold your dream close to your heart.

Sometimes our dreams don't birth in the spring season, summer season, fall season, or winter season, but sometimes they come into fruition in the fifth season—the due season. "And let us not grow weary while doing good, for in due season we shall reap if we do not lose heart" (Gal. 6:9).

I can't begin to tell you how many times I've held on to Galatians 6:9. I went through many dark seasons, lonely seasons, and testing seasons before my dreams began to birth. One of many things that kept me motivated was my dream-picture book, which I highly recommend you create for your destiny potential, but you must have the will to act on what you believe about your dream.

Do you remember the old saying "a picture is worth a thousand words"? A dream-picture scrapbook, a dream-picture photo album, or dream-picture poster board with various pictures of the future you desire is a simple but powerful strategy to keep your dreams always before you, reminding you to press on, that your dream can be a reality.

Find some used, outdated magazines and cut out any pictures that identify with your destiny. Take pictures of the dream car you would like to own someday or the neighborhood you want to live in and print them. Visit the Websites of the companies you'd like to work for or the university you would like to attend. Print out those pictures. Collect those pictures and place them in a photo album or tape them in a notebook or journal. Never limit your pictures; keep placing as many pictures that support the dream you desire, even those things that seem far-fetched. This dream booklet or dream photo album is an inexpensive way to keep your dream alive.

Your dream-picture book will take you closer to and eventually help you reach your goals, but look through your dream-picture book regularly, even every day. Let your eyes see what you desire for your future.

Pray over your dream-picture book morning and night, asking God to help them become a reality.

As you repeat this each day, you will begin to imagine yourself living your dream life. Have fun with this, share it with your close friends and family, use this as yet another avenue to keep motivated on your journey toward your goals. Once you begin to gain some small wins with your dream-picture book, you'll be motivated to continue moving forward toward your destiny.

Your dream-picture book will help you stay focused, committed; and it will hold you accountable. When you feel the momentum slipping, viewing your dream-picture book will encourage you to create action plans, which will bring tangible results.

The purpose of your dream-picture book is to inspire you as you take each action step that is necessary to reach your goal. Always look to God to help you materialize your dreams.

Takeaway Points

Never quit on your dream.

Do not let a lack of finances stop you from dreaming.

People laugh at great dreams and great dreamers.

Your dream-picture book will help you stay focused, committed, and accountable.

Questions to Reflect On

If you knew your dreams could not fail, what would be your biggest dream?

Why do most people's dreams lie dormant?

Why is the process from dream to reality so difficult?

What has God been telling you lately about your dream? What do you need to do as a result of that message?

3

The Will to Win

You have to know you can win.
You have to think you can win.
You have to feel you can win.

—Sugar Ray Leonard

Patrick "Pat" James Riley is an American professional basketball executive, and a former coach and player in the NBA. Currently, he is team president of the Miami Heat. Widely regarded as one of the greatest NBA coaches of all time, Riley has served as the head coach of five championship teams. In 1996 he was named one of the 10 Greatest Coaches in the NBA history. Riley most recently won the 2012 NBA Championship with the Miami Heat as their team president. This made him the first (and so far only) NBA figure to win an NBA championship as a player, coach (both assistant and head), and executive.

Pat Riley is a winner. As the head coach of the NBA Champions Los Angeles Lakers, Pat Riley predicted that his team would win back-to-back championships.

At the celebration following the Lakers' 1987 title, Coach Pat Riley guaranteed—not predicted, but guaranteed—a repeat championship in '88, a feat that had not been accomplished in eighteen NBA seasons.

"Guaranteeing a championship was the best thing Pat ever did," reflected Lakers guard Byron Scott. "It set the stage in our minds. Work harder, be better. That's the only way we could repeat [the championship]."

The Los Angeles Lakers played through the 1987–88 season with even more pressure than usual for the NBA defending champion.

The Lakers marched to the NBA Finals, where they went up against the talented and hungry Detroit Pistons, who had finally gotten past rival Boston to appear in their first Finals.

The Pistons surprised the Lakers by winning Game 1 at The Forum and held a 3–2 lead heading back to Los Angeles following a 104–94 win before 41,732 fans at the Pontiac Silverdome.

But with the last two games on their home turf, the Lakers made good on Riley's brash guarantee. They survived a 25-point third-quarter explosion by Isiah Thomas, playing on a sprained ankle, no less, to take Game 6 (103–102). Then they won Game 7 (108–105) to capture their fifth championship of the 1980s.

In his book *The Winner Within You: A Life Plan for Team Players,* Pat Riley wrote, "You have no choice about how you lose, but you do have a choice about how you come back and prepare to win again." To win you must purposefully and intentionally devise a winning game plan. You must be consistent as you establish the habits that will aid you as you work toward your goals. You must develop and follow a well-thought-out and practical strategy.

See yourself a winner. Develop a vision of your desired future. Albert Einstein said, "Your imagination is your preview of life's coming attraction." Just because you have not yet arrived at your destination does not mean you can't live a life of destiny.

Destiny is not just a location but also a state of mind.

Destiny is a predetermined triumph. When you live a life of destiny, you are living life in the winning column. Winners sometimes lose but they never whine. Just because you've lost doesn't mean you are a loser; it just means you've lost that particular battle. Manuel Diotte said, "Winning isn't always finishing first, sometimes winning is just finishing."

At the 1992 Summer Olympic Games in Barcelona, Spain, Derek Redmond of Great Britain was running the men's 400 meters semifinal when all of sudden he tore his hamstring. He fell in pain. His father ran to his side. Derek got up and told his father, "I've got to finish this race."

His father said, "If you're gonna finish the race, we'll finish it together."

Derek, with assistance from his father, managed to limp and hobble a full lap around the track. He made it to the finish as the crowd gave him a standing ovation. What a win! Winning is sometimes perseverance, enduring, and keeping a winning attitude.

Whenever you finish a project, that's a win; when you finish another semester in school, that's a win; when you finish paying off one debt, that's a win; when you finish the diet, that's a win; when you finish the business plan, that's a win;

when you finish writing a chapter in your book, that's a win. Many of us have started, but very few of us finish what we've started. Anybody can start, but it takes a winner to finish. Albert Gray was right on point when he said, "Winners have simply formed the habit of doing things losers don't like to do."

Develop a Winning Attitude

These are my 12 Characteristics of People with a Winning Attitude

1. They are self-driven
2. They self-motivated
3. They have a positive self-image
4. They are self-determined
5. They are lifelong learners
6. They have a teachable spirit
7. They are team players
8. They are courageous and bold
9. They are self-disciplined
10. They are optimistic
11. They are dependent on God's strength
12. They speak positive affirmations over their lives

In the words of Lou Houltz, "Winning is never accidental." The Bible says, "Yet in all these things we are more than conquerors through Him who loved us" (Rom. 8:37).

We know a winner when we see one. True winners never give up or give in. They don't know how to quit. True winners hate to lose. When you lose, you feel the agony of defeat and anguish of disappointment, but sometimes living involves losing. Jackie Robinson once said, "Above anything else, I hate to lose."

The fact is sometimes you lose. But the most important thing we need to remember is that in our defeats, we can learn more from losing than from winning; we can learn more from failing than from succeeding. John Maxwell said, "Sometimes you lose, sometimes you learn." The key is not to focus so much on losing but learning from losing. Wilma Rudolph said, "Winning is great, sure, but if you are really going to do something in life, the secret is learning how to lose. Nobody goes undefeated all the time. If you can pick up after a crushing defeat, and go on to win again, you are going to be a champion someday."

We must learn from our defeats and never adopt a victim's mentality.

One of the negative qualities of losers is that they develop a victim mind-set. They make excuses for not having the will to win.

Their motto is If Only:

If only my parents weren't divorced
If only I wasn't single
If only I was rich
If only I wasn't handicapped
If only I wasn't abused
If only I had a college education
If only I had a better job
If only I hadn't gotten pregnant out of wedlock
If only I didn't go bankrupt

Whatever you do, don't be an "If Only Victim." Come to your senses and say, "God has made me to win." The Bible tells a story of the Two Lost Sons, famously known as The Prodigal

Son. It is one of the parables of Jesus. According to the gospel of Luke (15:11–32), a father gives in to the demands of his younger son and hands over his share of his inheritance. The younger son leaves home and quickly wastes his fortune in fast living. (The word *prodigal* means "wastefully extravagant.") With his money gone he finds work slopping pigs. He's so hungry the pig slop looks good to him.

I can imagine this young man's living conditions, because when I was in the fourth grade, my very first job was working for our neighbor across the street. Mr. Aldridge raised hogs. It was a sloppy, stinking job with very little pay—$1.00 a week with no benefits.

This young man in Luke's gospel lost his focus and his relationship with his father, which led him to live a defeated life. Can't you see him crawling on his hands and knees in the muck? Picking through the slop, hoping to find some morsel to quit the aching in his empty stomach. But something good happened: broke, busted, and disgusted, he saw his dire need and came to his senses. It was there that he took inventory: he assessed his situation; then he decided to do the right thing and go back home, no matter what status he might be lowered to. It was in the pigpen that he made a most important decision. He said, "I will (the power of his will) set out and go back to my Father and say to Him, 'Father, I have sinned against heaven and against you.'" If he had not used the will that God gave him, he would have died from starvation and lack.

Whenever you hook up with God, it's always a win. Many of us have family and friends who are sitting in pigpen dilemmas right now. In their own minds they are "as happy as pigs in slop," as the saying goes. Oh, if they would declare and decree, like the young prodigal, that I will, I can, I shall, I must arise up out of the slop of self-pity and self-defeat into a lifestyle of winning.

In 1989 Jimmy Johnson was to be the new head coach of the Dallas Cowboys, replacing Tom Landry, who had coached the team since its beginning in 1960. In Johnson's first season as coach, the 1989 Cowboys went 1–15. Johnson, however, did not take long to develop the Cowboys into a championship-quality team. Over the next four to five years, Johnson coached the Cowboys to consecutive Super Bowl wins: Super Bowl XXVII in 1992 and Super Bowl XXVIII in 1993. Jimmy Johnson said, "The difference between ordinary and extraordinary is that little extra." That little extra sacrificing, that little extra effort, that little extra push, that little extra praying, that little extra studying, that little extra willpower can propel you to your greatest victories.

In 1952 Edmund Hillary attempted to climb Mount Everest but failed. A few weeks later a group in England asked him to address its members. Edmund Hillary walked onstage to thunderous applause. The audience was recognizing him because he had attempted greatness. But Hillary saw himself as a failure. He walked away from the microphone and to the edge of the platform. He made a fist and pointed at a picture of the mountain. He said in a loud voice, "Mount Everest, you beat me the first time, but I'll beat you the next time, because you've grown all you are going to grow . . . and I'm still growing!"

One of the keys to growing in life is never to settle because of a defeat, a loss, or a setback. The more you know, the more you grow in your field of expertise. Someone once said that your attitude will determine your altitude.

Your attitude determines your actions.

Who hasn't read the beloved story of *The Little Engine that Could*? One day a long train of freight cars needed to be pulled over the next hill. The train asked one large engine to pull it, but the engine said no. The train asked another engine that also refused. The train asked engine after engine, each one turning it down. Finally, the train came to the little switch engine and asked it to pull the freight train over the hill. The little engine said, "I think I can," and took the position at the head of the train. The little engine pulled the freight train, but when it saw the hill, it knew it would be hard work. Not to give up so easily, the little train puffed and puffed, telling itself, "I think I can. I think I can." Halfway up the hill the little engine began to struggle and puffed harder. But it kept saying, "I think I can. I . . . think . . . I can." Nearing the top and barely moving, it refused to give up. "I . . . think . . . I . . . can." As soon as it topped the hill and began the downward trek, it said, "I thought I could. I thought I could."

The little engine had to labor to pull the freight train, but it determined to complete the job. You must think you can win. "For as a man thinks in his heart so is he" (Prov. 23:7 KJV).

The Chinese bamboo tree grows in Asia Minor. It starts with a little seed. You plant it, water it, and fertilize it for a whole year, and nothing happens. The second year you water it and fertilize it, and nothing happens. The third year you water it and fertilize it, and still nothing happens. This becomes discouraging! But you persist. The fourth year you water it and fertilize it, and nothing happens. Frustrating. The fifth year you continue to water and fertilize the seed and then . . . the Chinese bamboo tree spouts and grows ninety feet in six weeks!

Life is akin to the growing process of the Chinese bamboo tree. It is often discouraging. We seemingly do things right and nothing happens. But for those who do things right and persist, even if they are discouraged and frustrated, things will happen. Finally, we begin to receive the rewards.

In the pursuit to win and become more, you will have problems. Welcome to Life 101.

If you think you are going to win in life without any problems, you had better prepare for a rude awakening.

Problems are part of life.
Problems are inescapable.
Problems can destroy us or develop us.
Problems can hurt us or help us.
Problems can make us bitter or better.

God gave Noah instructions to build an ark and prepare for a major flood that would result because of forty straight days and nights of rain. Even Noah had problems. The old poem goes like this:

When Noah sailed the ocean blue,
He had problems the same as you,
For forty days he drove the ark,
Before he found a place to park.

God will always make sure you have a place to park. God helped Noah and his family win through the forty-day storm. Dolly Parton once said, "If you want to get to the end of the rainbow, you must be willing to put up with the rain."

So before you get to your destiny, start talking like a winner, walking like a winner, dressing like a winner, planning like a winner. Arthur Ashe said, "Regardless of how you feel inside, always try to look like a winner. Even if you are behind, a sustained look of control and confidence can give you a mental edge that results in victory."

If the old saying is true that birds of a feather flock together, then winning people connect with other winning people. Big thinkers are attractive to other big thinkers. Keep winning people in your circle. Keep people with goals, dreams, and integrity in your circle. Keep people who are driven, focused, and generous in your circle.

Keep negative people, who often complain and whine about life, far from your circle. The old saying is true, "Misery loves company." Negative people can become toxic waste in your life. Whether they are family, friends, coworkers, or neighbors, make the tough decision to separate from negativity.

It reminds me of the story "The Eagle Who Almost Was":

> Once upon a time, an eagle's nest rested on a large mountainside. The eagle's nest contained four large eagle eggs. One day an earthquake rocked the mountain, causing one of the eggs to roll down the mountain to a chicken farm in the valley below. The chickens knew that they must protect and care for the eagle's egg, so an old hen volunteered to nurture the large egg.
>
> One day, the egg hatched and a beautiful eagle emerged. Sadly, however, the hen raised the eagle as a chicken. The eagle believed he was nothing more than a chicken. The eagle loved his home and family, but his spirit cried out for more.
>
> While playing a game on the farm one day, the eagle looked to the skies above and noticed a group of mighty eagles soaring in the skies. "Oh," the eagle cried, "I wish I could soar like those birds."

The chickens roared with laughter. "You cannot soar with those birds. You are a chicken and chickens do not soar."

The eagle continued staring at his real family up above, dreaming that he could be with them. Each time the eagle spoke his dream, the chickens said it couldn't be done. That is what the eagle learned to believe. The eagle, after time, stopped dreaming and continued to live his life like a chicken. Finally, after a long life as a chicken, the eagle passed away.

The moral of the story: You become what you believe you are. So if you ever dream to become an eagle, follow your dreams, not the words of a chicken.

The little eagle let the negativity of the chickens influence him, and he forfeited his destiny to fly. Negative toxic-waste people can be an irritation to your life. If you let them, they will disrupt your happiness, interfere with your productivity, and basically become a major issue to deal with. If you are not careful, they can turn your happy day into barbaric pain. They will talk you out of your dreams and keep you stuck in the cement of fear. Implement some or all of these recommendations to protect yourself against negative people:

- Change your cell number
- Tell them you can't hang out anymore
- Set firm boundaries (not allow toxic people to use you)
- Refuse to listen to them complain
- Refuse to bail them out of repeated trouble
- Fire them out of your life if necessary
- Pray for their change

> *You are who you hang out with. You become like the people you keep in your circle.*

Negative, toxic people will zap your energy, take the fun out of life, and make you become like them. Toxic-waste people have something in common: they're all unhappy, wounded people. They have never dealt with their hidden hurts. As the old saying goes, "Hurt people hurt people." A recent study demonstrated that a whopping 97 percent of society is fueled by negativity. We may live in a negative world, but we control what we allow into our minds. You can't control what other people say or do, but you can control what you let into your mind and who you let into your life. Choose to ignore negativity or to let it eat you alive. As the old song goes, "You've got to accentuate the positive, eliminate the negative . . . and don't mess with Mister In between."

One reason why negative people try to pull you down is because you are already above them. If you allow them to pull you down to their level, you will find yourself wallowing in the muck of defeat and negativity. James Altucher said, "When you get in the mud with a pig, you get dirty and the pig gets happy."

Don't make your haters happy; don't make their wish of bringing you down come true.

Nehemiah, a cupbearer, left a comfortable job as an assistant to the king of Persia in order to help the demoralized people of Jerusalem. Nehemiah demonstrated that with God's help you can overcome negativity. Nehemiah was courageous in dealing with opposition. Sanballat, Geshem, and Tobiah opposed the rebuilding of Jerusalem's walls and mocked the work of God's people.

Nehemiah replied to his critics, "I am doing a great work, so that I cannot come down. Why should the work cease while I leave it and go down to you?" (Neh. 6:3).

In other words, don't come down off your wall of purpose and productivity for foolishness and folly, because if you do, you will play into the hands of your haters. You must do what Nehemiah did: stay on the top of your dreams, your finances, your family, your goals, and your future.

Toxic people are haters in disguise.

Mark Twain once said, "Keep away from people who try to belittle your ambitions. Small people always do that, but the really great make you feel that you, too, can become great."

Stay on your wall, for you have no time for nonsense and stupidity. If you are trying to win, and I know that you are, stay on the wall. Keep working, keep learning, keep growing, and keep praying, because success is just a matter of time.

Nehemiah finished rebuilding the wall. You too must finish what you started, and don't sweat the negative stuff people say and do. Oliver Cromwell said, "He who stops being better stops being good."

"A man is not old until regrets take the place of dreams."
—John Barrymore

Takeaway Points

Develop a winning attitude.
Winners sometimes lose, but they never whine.

The more you know, the more you grow in your field of expertise.

Negative people try to pull you down because you are already above them.

Questions to Reflect On

What have I naturally won at in the past?
What do I naturally do well?
What excites me about life?
What do others say makes me unique?

4

The Will to Develop Your Mind

A mind once stretched never returns to its original state.
—Oliver Wendell Holmes

Growing up in the '70s, one of our Saturday traditions was to watch *Soul Train*, the American musical variety show that featured performances by R&B, soul, and hip hop artists, which sometimes included funk, jazz, disco, and gospel artists as well. It was during one of those *Soul Train* episodes that I saw one of the most powerful commercials I had ever witnessed. In it a young black male teenager has a chance to go to college. As he prepares to hop onto the bus to attend school, he realizes he lacks funding. So he gets off the bus, missing out on an opportunity of a lifetime. The commercial would end with the slogan that has been used for years by the United Negro College Fund, "A mind is a terrible thing to waste." The point of the commercial was that there were many highly qualified and motivated black students who couldn't attend college without some sort of financial aid, and that bright kids were missing opportunities and falling through the cracks for lack of funds.

Your mind decides what level of health, happiness, and wealth you have. It influences your relationships, your physical fitness, your weight, your income, your savings, your satisfaction. To a certain degree, it controls the success you have in everything. Your mind controls everything you do, and it also controls the results you get in your life. You can have a lazy mind-set, a poverty mind-set, a defeated mind-set, a victim mind-set—it's your choice. You can have a driven mind-set, a spiritual mind-set, a prosperous mind-set, a winning mind-set, a positive mind-set—and that's your choice as well. But if you want different results in your life, you must be willing to change your mind-set.

You are where you start out by chance, but you are where you end up by choice.

William James wrote in *The Principles of Psychology,* "Man alone, of all creatures of the earth, can change his own pattern. Man alone is the architect of his destiny. The greatest discovery in our generation is that human beings, by changing the inner attitudes of their minds, can change the outer aspects of their lives."

It amazes me that in my late teens and early twenties, my thinking and mind-set were limited, confined to my environment. I can say that I am no longer bound by what I can see. My vision and mind-set are no longer restricted.

How do you keep the mighty elephant tied down? When a baby elephant is tied to a stick in the ground, it is not strong enough to pull away, though it tries and tries and tries. After a while, it gives up and believes it is stuck. By the time the elephant is an adult, it still believes that the stick holds it in place, even though the elephant is more than capable of breaking away. In other words, the elephant has been programmed to think that it is limited because of the limitations placed on it as an infant. Don't let any limitations in your childhood and early environments stop you from breaking free.

Quick question: What limitations have you placed on your life?

Dr. Vincent Fortanasce wrote,

> Studies show that people who have a higher education or continue to learn throughout their lives may be at lower risk of Alzheimer's disease than those who have less education. Please note that by education, researchers are not referring to the number of years of formal education.... People who continue to learn— by traveling to new places, reading books, visiting art galleries and museums, and discussing their finding with family and friends, doing crossword puzzles daily, playing a musical instrument or learning a new language—boost the size of their brain reserve and reduce their chance of Alzheimer's disease.[1]

What limits have you put on your mind? What restrictions have you put on your mind? I highly recommend that you continue to develop your mind. Dream big dreams, have big goals, and set high standards for yourself.

It's not a sin to dream big.

Benjamin Elijah Mays, former president of Morehouse College said,

It must be borne in mind that the tragedy of life doesn't lie in not reaching your goal. The tragedy lies in having no goal to reach. It isn't a calamity to die with dreams unfulfilled, but it is a calamity not to dream. It is not a disaster to be unable to capture your ideal, but it is a disaster to have no ideal to capture. It is not a disgrace not to reach the stars, but it is a disgrace to have no stars to reach for. Not failure, but low aim is sin.[2]

Sometimes I get to visit friends from the urban neighborhood, often referred to as the hood, where I grew up. I see many who fell through the cracks of life. I see many on the same corner, in the same conversation, playing the same games, living the same core values—wasting their gifts, talents, and potential. There's no conversation about God, dreams, finances, family, or education. Mostly, it's about the old days, shooting hoops, chasing skirts, getting high, and drinking malt liquor. For the most part, nothing has changed in their lives but the years. That's one of the purposes for my writing this manual for living. It is to wake up somebody who's among the living dead. I want everyone who's reading this manual to know that there's a dream in you, a book in you, a ministry in you, a business in you, a nonprofit in you, and perhaps a school in you. For some who are reading this book, there's art in you, music in you, dance in you, innovation in you, and perhaps creativity in you.

Shift your mind-set and begin to think positive, productive, and purposeful thoughts.

The Reverend Floyd Flake, a former U.S. congressman from Queens, New York, is an African American hero in the tradition of great black leaders who worked with all that was available to them, surpassing both racism and low expectations. Flake describes bootstrapping as "a process of achieving success by making it against the odds, through self-directed action. It is a mind-set that allows you to rise over and above the ordinary and become an extraordinary person by taking responsibility for your thoughts." I like the bootstrap philosophy, but, truth be told, I didn't have any boots or straps, yet I made up my mind and will to go above mediocrity.

Your perspective and viewpoint must always look at life from God's perspective. I believe that one's up-look can affect his or her outlook. Frederick Langbridge said, "Two men look out the same prison bars; one sees mud and the other sees stars."

One had an upward attitude and the other a downward attitude.

Charles Swindoll said a mouthful when talked about the importance of attitude.

> The longer I live, the more I realize the impact of attitude on life. Attitude, to me, is more important than facts. It is more important than the past, than education, than money, than circumstances, than failures, than successes, than what other people think or say or do. It is more important than appearance, giftedness or skill. It will make or break a company... a church... a home.
>
> The remarkable thing is we have a choice every day regarding the attitude we will embrace for that day. We cannot change our past.... we cannot change the fact that people will act in a certain way. We cannot change the inevitable. The only thing we can do is play on the one string we have, and that is our attitude.... I am convinced that life is 10% what happens to me and 90% how I react to it.

And so it is with you.... we are in charge of our attitudes.[3]

We can change our lives by changing our attitudes. Begin this day to look at life through a new set of lenses.

You can choose to

- get better or bitter
- develop or decline
- get healthy or stay unhealthy
- get out of debt or stay in debt
- become educated or have limited education
- grow or stay stuck

It's your choice. I believe if you change your thinking, it brings your preferable future into the realm of possibilities. Henry Ford, the founder of the Ford Motor Company, once said, "If you think you can or if you think you can't, you're right."

I am encouraging you through the words on this page to begin to think you can and to begin to think you will. Dr. Norman Vincent Peale said, "You are not what you think you are. But what you think." To believe that you can become more will break and demolish the limitations on your mental faculties. When you possess an "I can do" optimistic attitude, it jolts your spirit and sets off an abrupt spasmodic movement in your soul so that your synapses begin to fire. Why? Because a breakthrough has taken place and a new discovery in your mind occurs. You are now able to penetrate the barriers that held you back.

At this moment I CAN becomes more important than IQ. You have now ignited a new fire, a new spark that excites you about the next chapter of your life. If these pages you're reading inspire you and give you hope about becoming more than you are, you will soon overflow with enthusiasm. Samuel Ullman made a powerful statement: "Time will wrinkle the skin, but a life without enthusiasm will wrinkle the soul." Be excited about today, about this moment, about your future, about the possibilities.

The 1989 film *Dead Poet's Society* tells the story of English professor John Keating, who inspires his students at Welton Academy to a love of poetry and teaches them to overcome their reluctance to make their lives count. Professor Keating would often quote *carpe diem*, which means "seize the day." We should seize the day and make the most of each day, because we never know when it's our last day.

This moment right now is a pregnant moment in your life, a destiny moment. Take advantage of this moment, this opportunity, and this day.

Today can be first day of the best of your life. Make the next years of your life the best years of your life.

You can use many poor, weak excuses to keep you stuck and inferior. You can also break through any of the above excuses (barriers) to a wonderfully productive mind-set. Get rid of any stinking thinking that has held you back, and prepare to break through your mental limitations. To think is to reason, to ponder, and to analyze. Now imagine the possibilities of your life excelling and surpassing your excuses, your pain, and your failures. Improve your life by improving your thinking.

When you break through the status quo and develop a new mental paradigm, you reinvent your thinking by training your mind. I agree with Thomas Edison when he said, "If we did all the things we are capable of doing, we would literally astound ourselves."

What are some ways you can develop your mind?

- Pray.
- Read the Bible, inspirational books, and biographies of successful people.
- Read with a dictionary and thesaurus close by to look up unfamiliar words.
- Use a pen or pencil and highlighter to mark significant passages.
- Keep notes in a notepad, journal, or electronic tablet.
- Reflect on what you read.
- Find a quiet place to think.
- Blog and journal.
- Listen to personal-growth podcasts.
- Write down quotes from what you read.
- Do crossword or jigsaw puzzles.
- Solve math problems.
- Take a course on personal development and leadership.

Takeaway Points

Your mind decides what level of health, happiness, and wealth you have.

Big thinkers are attractive to big thinkers.

You must first think you can and think you will.

This moment right now is a pregnant moment in your life, a destiny moment.

Questions to Reflect On

What limitations have you placed on your life?

In what ways will you challenge yourself?

What negative attitudes will you release from your life?

The Will To Be

Do you make excuses for your limitations?

Do you ever tell yourself any of these excuses?

- I'm too old.
- I'm too young.
- I'm not educated.
- I'm financially broke.
- I'm not self-motivated.
- I'm not as gifted.
- I'm too undisciplined.

5

The Will to Plan Your Life

You were born to win, but to be a winner, you must plan to win, prepare to win, and expect to win.

—Zig Ziglar

Many people are living their lives on accident rather than on purpose. This purposeless living is many times due to a lack of planning and a lack of praying. We cannot coast through life aimlessly, without a sense of direction, if we are to fulfill our destinies. We must have a road map, a compass, a blueprint, a guideline, or a rough draft to help us chart a projective, possible, and fulfilling life. With a plan of action you can draft a diagram of where you would like to be in the next few months, years, or decades. A plan helps you to measure your progress toward your desired future.

Purposeful living is planned living.

I also believe that wasted living is unplanned and unprayerful living. With a plan we are more likely to succeed in our endeavors, ventures, and exertions. If you fail to plan, you plan to fail. Well-known author on personal time management Alan Lakein said, "Planning is bringing the future into the present so you can do something about it now." Planning your life means starting right now, today, this minute, this second . . . without delay. God has plans for us, yet how dare we make no plans for ourselves. "'For I know the plans I have for you,' declares the LORD, 'plans to prosper you and not to harm you, plans to give you hope and a future'" (Jer. 29:11).

Take charge of your life and create a sense of urgency. If you've wasted time in the past like me, I recommend that you act speedily, quickly, and promptly to maximize the time you have left on earth. I tell people that I'm a late bloomer but at least I'm blooming. Stop making excuses and start making adjustments. Poor excuses do not make a rich, purposeful life.

An excuse is a substitute for a lack of discipline and a lack of planning.

When we plan, we are more likely to get to our destinies. The American financier, banker, and art collector John Pierpont Morgan once said, "The first step towards getting somewhere is to decide you're not going to stay where you are." You have to make up your mind that you are not going to stay on Mediocre Boulevard and Complacent Avenue. It's your choice! Now choose to plan. You can chose or lose, it's your choice.

Where would you like to be five years from today?

The Will To Be

Where would you like to be ten years from today?
What is your plan?
What goals have you set for the following areas of your life?

- Faith
- Family
- Financials
- Fitness
- Fun
- Future

How will you set goals to see your plan become a reality? It is a fact that 95 percent of Americans do not have written goals.

You must have goals to know where you're going and how you'll get there. Hal Urban stated, "Living without goals is like going on a trip without a destination." Goals give us a sense of purpose, goals challenge us, goals discipline us, and goals make life much more fulfilling.

In the book *What They Don't Teach You in the Harvard Business School*, Mark McCormack tells of a study conducted on students in the 1979 Harvard MBA program. The students were asked, "Have you set clear, written goals for your future and made plans to accomplish them?" Only 3 percent of the graduates had written goals and plans; 13 percent had goals, but they were not in writing; and a whopping 84 percent had no specific goals at all.

Ten years later, the members of the class were interviewed again, and the findings, while somewhat predictable, were nonetheless astonishing. The 13 percent who had goals were earning, on average, twice as much as the 84 percent who had no goals at all. And what about the 3 percent who had clear, written goals? They were earning, on average, *ten times* as much as the other 97 percent put together. The group that had written goals became far more productive and successful.[1]

Brian Tracy said, "Goals in writing are dreams with deadlines." Earl Nightingale adds to this idea with, "People with goals succeed because they know where they're going."

Set SMART[2] goals. There are many variations of what SMART stands for, but the essence is this—goals should be:

- Specific
- Measurable
- Attainable
- Relevant
- Time-Bound

Set Specific Goals

Your goal must be clear and well-defined. Make it as easy as you can to get where you want to go by defining precisely where you want to end up.

Set Measurable Goals

Include precise amounts, dates, and so on in your goals so you can measure your degree of success.

Set Attainable Goals

Make sure that it's possible to achieve the goals you set, while not making them too easy to reach, either. Your goals should require you to raise the bar, and by this you will be most fulfilled when you achieve them.

Set Relevant Goals

Goals should be relevant to the direction you want your life and career to take. By keeping goals aligned with this, you'll develop the focus you need to get ahead and do what you want.

Set Time-Bound Goals

You goals must have a deadline. This will motivate you to stay focused, work with a sense of urgency, and finish strong.

Write your goals on paper and post them in visible places to remind yourself every day of what you intend to do. Put them on your walls, desk, computer monitor, bathroom mirror, or refrigerator as a constant reminder. Share them with other family members and coworkers.

Make an Action Plan

This is one of the most important steps while setting goals, but is often skipped. You get so focused on the final outcome that you forget to plan all of the necessary steps along the way. By writing out each step, you can track your progress and mark off each one as you complete it—and get more excited as you get closer to fulfilling your goals.

A 6-Step Process to Plan Your Life

- Pray
- Plan
- Prepare

- Practice
- Patience
- Prosper

Plan to prosper or you can accidentally fail.

Many people fail simply because they don't have a plan to succeed or to prosper. I was one of those people who go through life without any goals or plans. One reason I didn't plan my life was that I just didn't know how, much less where to start. Leon Tec, MD, said, "A sailor without a destination cannot hope for a favorable wind."

I really didn't know that I could start by writing down one goal and working toward it. Sometimes it's what we don't know that keeps us stuck in the cement of mediocrity, that keeps us puzzled and baffled. Sometimes it's what we don't know that keeps us indefinite, undetermined, and ambivalent. Sometimes it's what we don't know that keeps us perplexed, hesitant, and indecisive. "My people are destroyed for lack of knowledge" (Hos. 4:6).

Denis Waitley, motivational speaker and author, said this about goals: "The reason most people never reach their goals is that they don't define them, or ever seriously consider them as believable or achievable. Winners can tell you where they are going, what they plan to do along the way, and who will be sharing the adventure with them."

Here's a big question that most people can't answer: Where are you going?

Set some low goals, some high goals, and then some BHAGs.

From Jim Collins and Jerry Porras's 1994 book *Built to Last*, we get the acronym BHAGs: Big Hairy Audacious Goals. BHAGs are tangible, energetic and highly focused. BHAGs are bigger, bolder, and more powerful than regular long- and short-term goals. BHAGs typically take years to fulfill.

You'll recognize these notable companies with BHAGs.

- Amazon: Aims to have every book ever printed in any language available in less than sixty seconds.
- Disney: Goal is to be the best company in the world for all fields of family entertainment.
- Google: Its objective is to organize the world's information and make it universally accessible and useful.
- Hong Kong Broadband Network: Targets to be the largest IP provider in Hong Kong by 2016.
- Microsoft: Goal is to have a computer on every desk and in every home.[3]

Now the question is, what are your BHAGs? Where do you see yourself in ten or fifteen years from today?

Jim Rohn once said, "Goals. There's no telling what you can do when you get inspired by them. There's no telling what you can do when you believe in them. There's no telling what will happen when you act upon them." There's no telling where your life can be five or ten years from today.

Samuel Insull said, "Aim for the top. There is plenty of room there. There are so few at the top it is almost lonely there." One reason it's lonely at the top is because most people never set goals to get to the top. They converse about it, they dream about it, but they never set goals to get there. Good intentions are not good enough. You need to make a pointed decision to set goals, work toward them, and finish them. You must strive and aspire to reach your goals.

I have many goals for my life, family, and ministry. For example, some of my personal-life goals include getting more spiritually and physically healthy in the next twelve months, to be more financially prepared for retirement in the next twenty-five to thirty years, to author ten to fifteen books over the next five years, to complete my Doctoral Degree in the next four years, to build my coaching network (Coach Me to Lead, which helps train and coach leaders, organizations, and individuals), and to help build a new campus for the ministry of Above & Beyond by 2015.

Notice two things about the goals for my personal life. First, each of my goals has a deadline. You must have a date or at least a year in mind in which you'd like to see your goals completed. Second, my personal goals are written down. According to Dave Kohl, professor emeritus at Virginia Tech, "People who regularly write down their goals earn nine times as much over their lifetimes as the people who don't." You must write down your goals and make them come alive.

When you write down your goals, you breathe life into them, and they become walking dreams.

The wisest man to ever live, King Solomon, wrote, "The plans of the diligent lead to profit as surely as haste leads to poverty" (Prov. 21:5 NIV). Keep dreaming, keep planning, keep strategizing, keep praying, and keep writing down your goals.

Og Mandino, in his miniature classic *The Greatest Secret in the World*, indicates the importance of sticking with your goal, step by step:

> The prizes of life are at the end of each journey, not near the beginning; and it is not given to me to know how many steps are necessary in order to

reach my goal. Failure I may still encounter at the thousandth step, yet success hides behind the next bend in the road. Never will I know how close it lies unless I turn the corner, always will I take another step, if that is of no avail I will take another, and yet another.... I will be liken to the rain drop which washes away the mountain; the ant who devours a tiger; the star which brightens the earth; the slave who builds a pyramid. I will build my castle one brick at a time for I know that small attempts, repeated, will complete ΛNY undertaking.[4]

Small attempts repeatedly, frequently, and regularly:
One hour a day for five days a week
Twenty hours a month
Two hundred forty hours a year

Make the commitment toward fulfilling one of your goals by putting in a little additional work every day. You will make progress like the turtle that makes progress when he stretches out his neck. My word of encouragement to you is to keep on stretching until you get to the finish line.

Plan your life starting now.

We have life insurance because we plan on dying, but few have a life plan because they don't plan on living. Don't just exist, live—but live with a plan. Be willing to take responsibility for the direction of your life by planning your life.

Takeaway Points

A plan helps you to measure your progress toward your desired future.

Stop making excuses and start making adjustments.

Good intentions are not good enough; you need to make a pointed decision to set goals and finish them.

God has plans for us, but how dare we make no plans for ourselves.

Questions to Reflect On

Where would you like to be five years from today?
Where would you like to be ten years from today?
What goals have you written down for this year?
Where are you going?

6

The Will to Be Your Best Version

Most of us live our entire lives as strangers to ourselves. We know more about others than we know about ourselves. Our true identity gets buried beneath the mistakes we've made, the insecurities we've acquired, and the lies we've believed.

—Mark Batterson

There's no one like you, never has been and never will be. A person can dress like you, walk like you, talk like you, even mimic you, but the fact is, they will never be you. Another truth is that you can never be someone else, because you were not made to copy someone else. You were not made to be a carbon copy. You were not made to duplicate but to innovate. When God made you, He set you apart from any other of His creation. There's only one you, and you need to be you and nobody else. Don't ever try to copycat someone else. You can learn from others and grow from others, but please

59

be you. Oscar Wild once said, "Be yourself because everyone else is taken."

Your uniqueness is different, your fingerprint is different, your DNA is different because God made you that way. I learned to accept my uniqueness, my distinctiveness, my brand of me. I am the one and only me, and that's the way God intended for it to be.

Dr. Dave Martin, in his book *The 12 Traits of the Greats*, wrote, "God understands your uniqueness, and He knows your potential. Unfortunately, too many of us have listened to our own voices or the voices of others. We have allowed others to identify us and to draw boundaries around our lives, and we have allowed our own misshapen thinking about ourselves to set artificial limitations upon us."

Often times we really don't understand who we are and Whose we are. Many individuals suffer an identity crisis because of low self-esteem or low self-worth. When we understand that we were created in the image of God, that alone should boost our self-esteem and self-worth. "So God created man in His own image; in the image [and likeness] of God created He him" (Gen. 1:27).

This same idea is seen in the popular T-shirt with a picture of the little kid that says, "I know I'm somebody because God doesn't make any junk."

John Ortberg wrote in his book *The Me I Want to Be*, "I am not all the me I want to be. You are not either. Both of us desire to become better people. But what does better mean? And how do we become better? The only way to become the person God made you to be is to live with the Spirit of God flowing through you like a river of living water."

When we understand that because God designed us, we are divinely designed, we should gain a better understanding of our roles with the gifts He has blessed each of us with.

Read this verse out loud: "I will praise you because I am fearfully and wonderfully made; your works are wonderful, I know that full well" (Ps. 139:14 NIV).

We are fearfully and wonderfully made. Wow! You are not too tall, not too short. You're not too wide, not too thin. You're not too light, not too dark. You are what God made you. You are divinely designed and fashioned with favor.

You are what you are by God's design as one of His prized possessions.

Jesus said that worrying about what you can't change about yourself is useless. Change what you can and accept what you can't. You can lose weight, but you can't get taller. Can the Ethiopian change his skin? No! You are what you are; it is what God says it is.

There's a story of a middle-aged woman who had a heart attack and was rushed to the emergency room. On the operating table she had a near-death experience. Seeing God, she asked if her time was up.

"No, you have another forty-three years, two months, and eight days to live," He said.

Upon recovery, she decided that because she had so much life remaining, she might as well make the most of it. So she stayed in the hospital and had a face-lift, liposuction, a tummy tuck—the whole works. She even had someone come in and change her hair color.

She was discharged after the final procedure; however, while crossing the street outside, she was killed by a speeding ambulance.

Arriving in God's presence, she fumed. "I thought You said I had another forty-plus years."

"I didn't recognize you," He said.

Stop being unhappy with yourself, and start praising God for your uniqueness.

John W. Gardner said, "Self-pity is easily the most destructive of the nonpharmaceutical narcotics; it is addictive, gives momentary pleasure and separates the victim from reality."

Many people have a problem with slipping into thinking of themselves as victims who have little or no control over their lives. In this headspace you feel sorry for yourself, develop a victim mentality, and think the world is against you. And you get stuck in that kind of thinking. You take little or no action, and you get lost in a funk of sadness and self-pity. Let me awaken you on this next statement: excuses are not an option.

Dr. Tim LaHaye lamented, "Every depressed person I have ever counseled has had a problem with self-acceptance." Did you catch the emphasis on the word *every*?

Along similar lines, Dr. James Dobson has noted: "In a questionnaire to young Christian mothers, their most common source of depression was clearly 'low self-esteem.' If I could write a prescription for the women of the world, it would provide each of them with a healthy dose of self-esteem and personal worth. I have no doubt that this is their greatest need."

Again, some of this lack of self-esteem can be tied to one's physical appearance. A survey taken a while back noted that 95 percent of all high school students and 100 percent of all movie stars would change something about their physical appearances if they could.

And then, according to the book *Inside America* by pollster Louis Harris, 99 percent of American women and 94 percent of American men would change something about their looks if possible.

Ann Landers lists problems with one's physical appearance—weight, birthmarks, baldness, height, etc.—as one of the ten most common problems people write to her about.

Someone wrote:

I think it would be lovely to live and do good,
To grow up to be the girl that I should;
A heart full of sunshine, a life full of grace
Are beauty far better than beauty of face.
I think it would be lovely to make people glad,
To cheer up the lonely, discouraged and sad;
What matter if homely or pleasant to see,
If lovely in spirit I'm striving to be.

Dr. Maxwell Maltz had a flourishing practice as a reconstructive and cosmetic facial surgeon, he lectured internationally on his medical specialty, and he pursued a dual career as a prolific author. He was inspired to move from treating "outer scars" to "inner scars" after observing that so many patients' unhappiness and insecurities were not cured with their newly reconstructed faces. "Dr. Maltz says that it is as if every personality has a face. This emotional face of personality seems to be the real key to change. If it remains scarred and distorted, ugly and inferior, then the person continues to act out a role, regardless of the change in his physical appearance. But if the face of his personality can be reconstructed, if the old emotional scars can be removed, the person can be changed.[1]

Our self-esteem influences our actions, behaviors, moods, and especially our relationships with other people.

While serving in Vietnam in 1969, Dave Roever nearly died when a phosphorus grenade exploded six inches from his right ear. He survived but was badly disfigured. In his talks on this experience, he describes his reunion with his pretty young wife, Brenda. "Brenda walked straight up to my bed, paused at the chart, read the tag on my arm, and, showing not the slightest tremor of horror or shock, bent over and kissed me on what was left of my face. Then she looked me in my good eye, smiled, and said: 'Welcome home, Davey. I love you!'

"All I could say was, 'I want you to know I'm real sorry.'

"She asked, 'Why are you sorry?'

"'Because I can never look good for you again.'

"She grinned and said, 'Oh, Davey, you never were good-looking anyway.'

"That was the beginning of the deep psychological and spiritual healing which eventually quenched the fire of my ordeal so I could face the world again."

Dave's wife looked past the scars and the missing parts of Roever's body to the abiding beauty that was still inside the husband that she loved.

Another wise person noted:

- At age twenty, we worry about what others think of us.
- At forty, we don't care what they think of us.
- At sixty, we discover that they haven't been thinking about us at all.

In short: look at others and be distressed; look at self and be depressed; look at Jesus and be blessed.

That is pretty good advice if you want to be one the most beautiful people in the world. Robert Browning, the famous English poet, wrote, "My business is not to remake myself, but to make the absolute best of what God made."

No one would consider the late Mother Teresa beautiful. And yet millions would agree that she was truly one of the most beautiful women of our time. Her inner beauty was so great it overwhelmed any physical deficiencies she might have had. That's why the old saying is true that you don't judge a book by its cover. "A beautiful woman who lacks discretion is like a gold ring in a pig's snout" (Prov. 11:22 NLT).

You can be pretty on the outside and ugly on the inside, and you're still pretty ugly.

It's been said, "Beauty is skin deep, but ugliness goes all the way to the bone." Make sure your beauty and good looks go deeper than your surface. A Ferrari is one of the most elegant cars in the world. Well-known and recognized, the Italian sports car is the top of its class. But if under the hood the motor is a lemon, a Ferrari is no good no matter how nice it looks. You don't want a good-looking Ferrari, you want a good-running Ferrari. Knowing who you are is important to becoming your best version of you.

When I was a little kid, I would put on my dad's shoes and clomp around the house. They were much too big for my feet, but I loved the feeling of walking in his shoes; I was fascinated with the ideal. The biggest reason my dad's shoes wouldn't fit was because they were not formed to my feet.

The person who walks in someone else's shoes never leaves his own footprints.

You are an original, the first you and the only you. You are rare, the exception to the rule. As much as I loved my dad, and as much as I loved walking in his shoes, I must walk in my own shoes, the pair God birthed on me at my birth. Now as a father, my son William J. Lindsey II may share my full name, but the truth is he could never be me, and someday if he has a son, his son could never be him. But each of us can be ourselves, and that's something nobody can beat us at.

Pablo Picasso, a Spanish painter, sculptor, printmaker, ceramicist, and stage designer who spent most of his adult life in France, was one of the greatest and most influential artists of the twentieth century. He said, "My mother said to me, 'If you become a soldier, you'll become a general; if you become a monk, you'll end up as the pope.' Instead, I become a painter and wound up as Picasso."

Many people never end up being themselves because they are so busy being who they are not and who they will never become.

"Please Hear What I'm Not Saying" is a poem by Charles C. Finn that warns against being fooled by the face, or mask, one wears. The poem talks about all people hiding behind masks to conceal the real us. He ends with these next few gripping lines:

Who am I, you may wonder?
I am someone you know very well.
For I am every man you meet
And I am every woman you meet.[2]

I'd rather be a real me than a fake somebody else.

You are a work of art, a poem in your own right, a masterpiece in God's eyes. Be willing not only to be yourself but also to be the best version of you that God made you to be. Take off the mask, quit pretending, and start being you.

I have often pondered what Patrick Rothfuss said: "We understand how dangerous a mask can be. We all become what we pretend to be." If this is true, then Robert Bloch's statement is even more interesting: "Horror is the removal of masks." Stop pretending and masquerading in the costume of somebody else. You are not somebody else. You are somebody: you are you. Be the best you and become your best version of you. When you die someday, die as an original not a cheap copy!

Takeaway Points

There's no one like you, never has been, and never will be.
You were not made to duplicate but to innovate.
Change what you can and accept what you can't.
Stop being unhappy with yourself and thank God for your uniqueness.

Questions to Reflect On

Do you know who you are?
Where do you get your self-worth?
Why do we wear masks?
What would the world miss if you weren't here?

7

The Will to Embrace
the Struggle

Your current struggle is building strength for your next season.
—William J. Lindsey

You always get the most use from a rubber band when you stretch it. I believe God gets our best when we are stretched, and sometimes our best requires that we strain, struggle, and sweat. Former slave and American social reformer, orator, writer, and statesman, Fredrick Douglass, said, "Where there is no struggle, there is no progress." Stress stretches us.

I think about the struggles of growing up in the hood, the urban inner-city community, trying not to fall through the cracks of life. I think about the struggles of going to six different elementary schools. I know the struggles of being in the fourth grade when I had to wear hand-me-down clothing that never fit. I remember the struggle of having to catch two metro buses after high school just to get to my part-time job on the other side of the city. I think about the struggle of going to summer school and night school just to finish my high school education, and attending six different colleges before finally completing my Bachelor of Science degree at the age of thirty-seven. I think about the struggle of being a young father with a wife and two young kids, working in a hot warehouse over two years without a raise. I think about the struggle of leading a non-growing church of five people for nearly three years before we saw any significant growth. That's a lot of Sundays in a row of struggling to grow the church past five members. I'm sure many people would not have lasted six months. I know about the struggles of pastoring one church with eight different locations before breaking ground on a new church campus. I know the struggles of trying to raise a family and maintain a healthy marriage. I know the struggles of trying to do right in a world filled with temptations to take shortcuts to the top.

The cool thing about my struggles is that I wouldn't give any of them back if I could. They served me in building character and courage into my life. They have made me stronger and wiser. They have kept me humble and hungry.

God allows struggles to help shape us and make us who we are.

I'm thankful that things didn't come easy for me. I'm thankful that I wasn't born with a silver spoon in my mouth. I'm thankful that my parents didn't spoil me and my siblings with everything we wanted. I'm grateful that I didn't ease on down the road. I'm here today because of the struggles, and I can truly say, they have built strength and endurance in my life.

You really don't know how strong you are until after the struggle. The old saying is "Hindsight is 20/20." When we look back over our personal struggles we endured, we can say they helped shaped us into the people we are.

Consider this illustration from nature. It's not easy to become an Emperor butterfly. To emerge into the world, it has to force its way through the neck of a flask-shaped cocoon. Getting through this opening takes hours of intense labor. The insect must squirm and wiggle and push its way through the confining threads. It is the struggle that makes the butterfly strong and viable. It is the pressure on the insect's body that forces essential chemicals into the wings that prepare it for flight. Without the struggle, it would never be able to fly or find food, and it would be vulnerable to predators. Its life would be short and miserable.

Sometimes, like the butterfly, we must squirm and wiggle and push our way through. We have to squirm, wiggle, push, and pray till we get to our destination. The truth is nobody told me the road would be easy.

Remember, the struggle is seasonal. Some seasons you will go through tough situations only to emerge stronger to handle the assignments and blessings God has for you in the next seasons.

One of the greatest lessons I've learned about life is that life is about seasons.

My father, the late Rev. John K. Lindsey, was a Baptist pastor, an entrepreneur, and a man with a serious work ethic. He would work hard from sunup to sundown six days a week. My mother, a homemaker until my late teen years, worked hard around the home, keeping it clean and preparing homemade meals daily. My siblings and I had chores every day after school. We raked the leaves in the yard, pulled weeds out of the flower bed, cleaned our rooms, and washed the dishes by hand—we called it busting suds. We learned early through our family business, Lindsey's Delivery Service, to work hard and don't look for handouts.

My parents taught us that no one will give you anything free, so you must work hard and make an honest living to earn your income. My father had a saying: "The early bird catches the worm." In other words, get up early and take advantage of the opportunities that each day brings. Benjamin Franklin was right when he wrote, "Early to bed and early to rise makes a man healthy, wealthy, and wise."

My father worked for a major antique company in the city of Houston, managed his own moving company, owned an antique shop, and pastored a church—all at the same time. He was not afraid of work. His father, my grandfather, the late William P. Lindsey, modeled a good work ethic. He had to hustle to make a living for his family. It was a struggle for my grandfather, my father, and me, but we knew how to get up and start running each day to provide for our families.

I'd like to share an African proverb, because it encapsulates the struggle in life.

Every morning in Africa, a gazelle wakes up. He has only one thought on his mind: to run faster than the fastest lion. If he cannot, he will be eaten. Every morning in Africa a lion awakens. He has only one thought on his mind: to run faster than the slowest gazelle. If he cannot, he will die of hunger. Whether you are chosen to be a gazelle or a lion is of no consequence. It is enough to know that with the rising of the sun, you must run. And you must run faster than you did yesterday or you will die. This is the race of life.

Get up and embrace the struggle. You can sweat and earn your way to a better life, or you can sit around and cry like a victim. African American civil rights activist Jesse Jackson stated, "Both tears and sweat are salty, but they render a different result. Tears will get you sympathy; sweat will get you change."

When you are faithful in small things, God will reward you with managing larger assignments. I've seen it in my own life. Being faithful over a handful of people in the church through the years has brought me to manage over a thousand people, leading them toward their spiritual and personal destinies. Hard work and an honest living got me where I am today. I do not believe in taking shortcuts. Although they may be tempting, trust me, it's not worth it. It's not worth losing your freedom, your family, your reputation, or God's favor over your life. So stay true to working, making wise choices and wise investments. Over the course of time, you'll get to the place you were meant to be.

Success comes from being faithful in small assignments.

"Life is hard by the yard, but inch by inch life's a cinch." Have you noticed that turtles beat the rabbits in races because the turtles keep moving forward at a steady pace while the rabbit scurries here and there? Before you know it, the turtle crosses the finish line to victory. How do you eat an elephant? One bite at a time. A journey of a million miles begins with the first step.

Vidal Sassoon said, "The only place where success comes before work is in the dictionary."

In 1962 Nelson Mandela was arrested and convicted of sabotage and other charges. He was sentenced to life in prison. Mandela served twenty-seven years in prison, spending many of these years on Robben Island. Following his release on February 11, 1990, Mandela led his party in the negotiations that resulted in multiracial democracy in 1994 in South Africa.

Nelson Mandela served as president of South Africa from 1994 to 1999, and was the first South African president to be elected in a fully representative democratic election. As president, he frequently gave priority to reconciliation, while introducing policies aimed at combating poverty and inequality in South Africa. Mandela said, "I had to suffer my way into leadership."

No matter what type of harsh treatment Mandela suffered, it did not break him. He had the will to be free. I've learned that you cannot lock up greatness, and that a man's gift will make room for him.

Robert Strauss said, "Success is a little like wrestling a gorilla. You don't quit when you're tired—you quit when the gorilla is tired." It reminds me of the story of the donkey that fell into the well. One day a farmer's donkey fell into a well. The farmer frantically thought what to do as the stricken animal cried out to be rescued. With no obvious solution, the farmer regretfully concluded that because the donkey was old, and the well needed to be filled in anyway, he should give up the idea of rescuing the beast and simply fill in the well. He hoped the poor animal would not suffer too much.

The farmer asked his neighbors to help, and before long they all began to quickly shovel earth into the well. When the donkey realized what was happening he wailed and struggled, but then, to everyone's relief, the noise stopped.

After a while the farmer looked down into the well and was astonished by what he saw. The donkey was still alive, and progressing toward the top of the well. The donkey had discovered that by shaking off the dirt instead of letting it cover him, he could keep stepping on top of the earth as the level rose. Soon the donkey was able to step up over the edge of the well, and he happily trotted off.

Life tends to shovel dirt on top of each of us from time to time. The trick is to shake it off and take a step up.

Shake off the lies people have told about you.
Shake off fear.
Shake off self-doubt.
Shake off self-pity.
Shake off false accusations.
Shake it off and put it under your feet.

Think about these authority figures and how they had to work through their struggles:

- Andrew Carnegie started work at $4 a month.
- John D. Rockefeller earned $6 a week.
- Julius Caesar was an epileptic.
- Napoleon ranked forty-sixth in his class of sixty-five.
- Beethoven was deaf.
- Thomas Edison was deaf as well.
- Charles Dickens was lame.
- Handel was lame as well.
- Homer was blind.
- Plato was a hunchback.
- Sir Walter Scott was lame.
- Demosthenes, the greatest orator of the ancient world, stammered.
- Abraham Lincoln was born in a log cabin, ridiculed for his appearance, and grew up in abject poverty.
- Franklin D. Roosevelt was struck with infantile paralysis.
- Glen Cunningham was burned so severely that doctors said he would never walk again, but he set the world's one-mile running record in 1934.
- Albert Einstein was written off as uneducable, a slow learner, and mentally retarded.
- Benson Idahosa was thrown onto the rubbish heaps, left to die because he was a sickly child.

- F. W. Woolworth built a great chain of department stores. Nevertheless, when he was twenty-one years old, his employers said he did not have sense enough to meet the public.
- When Walt Disney submitted his first drawings for publication, the editor told him he had no talent.

Lock him in a prison cell and you have a John Bunyan.

Bury him in the snows of Valley Forge, and you have a George Washington.

Amputate the cancer-ridden leg of a young Canadian, and you have a Terry Fox, who ran halfway across Canada on artificial legs.

Call him dull, hopeless, and flunk him out of school in the sixth grade, and you have the famous statesman Winston Churchill.

Take a man who did nothing wrong to anyone, and spit on Him, mock Him, humiliate Him, be His trusted friend and then completely betray Him and turn your back on Him, accept His loving kindness and service for years and then crucify Him, and after all this, have Him still forgive you, and raise from the dead after three days and you will have a Jesus of Nazareth, the Christ.[1]

Wilma Rudolph was born prematurely at 4.5 pounds, the twentieth of twenty-two children. Rudolph contracted infantile paralysis at age four. Her left leg and foot became twisted as a result, and she wore a brace until she was nine. By the time she was twelve years old she had also survived scarlet fever, whooping cough, chickenpox, and measles. Wilma embraced her struggle, and at the 1960 Summer Olympics in Rome, she won three Olympic titles. After this and several other wins, she gained notoriety as "the fastest woman in history." She was inducted into the U.S. Olympic Hall of Fame in 1983, honored with the National Sports Award in 1993, and inducted into the National Women's Hall of Fame in 1994.

All of these famous people pressed on through their trials and difficulties and gained victory in their lives. It would have been much easier for them if they had simply given up and let their troubles bury them. But they chose to follow their dreams and become the people they were meant to be.

What difficulties must you press through today to become the very best version of you?

Takeaway Points

You really don't know how strong you are until after the struggle.

You can sweat and earn your way to a better life, or you can sit around and cry like a victim.

A journey of a million miles begins with the first step.

You cannot lock up greatness.

A man's gift will make room for him.

Questions to Reflect On

What has been one of your biggest struggles?

What is the biggest thing you've learned from your struggle?

Are you faithful with your current daily assignments (whether work, education, or business)?

How many steps have you taken on the journey toward your destiny?

8

The Will to Develop Your Potential

The potential of the average person is like a huge ocean unsailed, a new continent unexplored, a world of possibilities waiting to be released and channeled toward some great good.

—Brian Tracy

The wealthiest place on planet Earth is not the diamond mines of South Africa, nor the Inca gold caches of Ecuador, nor the oil fields of Saudi Arabia, but, surprisingly, the graveyard. Whenever I go to the cemetery after a funeral service, I often look at the headstones and wonder if this person reached his or her destiny. Did this person fulfill her life calling? Did this person use all his potential? Did this person die a victim or a victor? On those headstones I see each person's full name, a birth date, and a death date. Between the birth date and death date is a dash that defines what each of those persons did with their lives.

The question is, what will you do with your dash?

Too many people have died with their dreams, visions, songs, poems, ministries, films, businesses, books, and aspirations unrealized, having contributed the best of themselves to the graveyard. My word to you is to encourage you not to be one of those who take their dreams to the grave.

You are pregnant with possibilities and potential. Many studies state that humans use only a small portion of their brains. To waste your God-given potential is a tragedy. It reminds me of the story by King Jaffe Joffer about the elderly man on his death bed.

> An elderly man, in the final days of his life, is lying in bed alone. He awakens to see a large group of people clustered around his bed. Their faces are loving, but sad. Confused, the old man smiles weakly and whispers, "You must be my childhood friends, come to say good-bye. I am so grateful." Moving closer, the tallest figure gently grasps the old man's hand and replies, "Yes, we are your best and oldest friends, but long ago you abandoned us. For we are the unfulfilled promises of your youth. We are the unrealized hopes, dreams, and plans that you once felt deeply in your heart, but never pursued. We are the unique talents that you never refined, the special gifts you never discovered. Old friend, we have not come to comfort you, but to die with you."[1]

This is the tragic story of too many people who have wasted sixty, seventy, or eighty years doing nothing.

> *We shouldn't just go through life;*
> *we should grow through life.*

Each year, each chapter, and each new season we should grow, learn, and experience more about God, life, people, and ourselves.

American psychologist and author William James said, "We are making use of only a small part of our possible mental and physical resources." You are not all you can be, and I'm not all I can be.

Potential is not what you are but what you can become. More than likely you are not using all of your potential. We have not tapped into all of our God-given potential. Just as a puppy has potential to become an adult dog, and a kitten has potential to become an adult cat, and a foal has potential to become an adult horse, we have potential to become whatever God has designed us to be.

We all have more potential and capacity that we have not yet used. Capacity is the ability to perform or produce. Capacity is innate potential for growth, development, or accomplishment. Capacity is simply stored potential. It's my willingness to be stretched, to grow, to expand, to extend myself, to spring up, and burst forth. Max Depree said, "In the end, it is important to remember that we cannot become what we need to be, by remaining what we are."

> *We should use our potential for a worthy*
> *cause, to make a difference, to change lives.*

In my early twenties I was stuck and limited in my mindset. I was working part-time at a K-Mart retail store, making minimum wage. Those were some hard times. I didn't have a car, so I had to walk two miles or hitch a ride just to get there.

During that season of my life, I would hang out with one of my best friends from high school and we would play Tecmo Bowl, a popular football arcade game. The game was so fun that we would play eight hours without a break—even to get food. Seriously! It was so much fun, but when I look back, I see that I wasted a lot of valuable time that I would never get back. I wasn't thinking about my career, education, and where I would like to be ten years from that day. I had no goals, no plans. I felt like I was stuck between a rock and a hard place. In spite of feeling stuck, I still had a will and a desire to be unstuck, I just didn't know how to go about it. No one in my family had attempted to go to college, talked about investments, or built wealth. My father had a successful business, but beyond that my vision for the future was shallow.

God has given each of us the power of a will and the potential to maximize all of our giftedness to a purposeful and fulfilling life. I learned that life doesn't have to be boring, tedious, and pointless. Life doesn't have to always be gloomy, bleak, and colorless.

Some people are stuck in life but don't know how to get unstuck.

You can be enthused about life. The word *enthusiasm* comes from two Greek words. The first word is *en*, "in," and the second is the word for "God": *theos*. It's the root for our word *theology*, the study of God or the doctrine of God. So whenever you get in God, you will be naturally enthused.

When you get in God, you will make adjustments to move forward toward a well-balanced, productive, progressive life. You give life all you have, and you hold nothing back.

Life is meant to be lived and explored.

Imagine that at the age of two you could no longer see, hear, or talk. Imagine the odds stacked against you. But also imagine you had the audacity to will your way to learn, to grow, and to win against your circumstances. Imagine if you willed your way into college, wrote nearly a dozen books, traveled all over the world, met twelve U.S. presidents, and lived to be eighty-seven. Well, there was such a person, an American author, political activist, and lecturer: Helen Keller, who as a toddler came down with scarlet fever that left her deaf and blind before she learned to speak. As a child, Helen was wild and unruly, and had little real understanding of the world around her. In March 1887, Miss Annie Sullivan, a twenty-year-old graduate of the Perkins School for the Blind, who had regained useful sight through a series of operations, came to the Kellers' home to help with Helen. Miss Sullivan saw Helen's potential to become more than the undisciplined child she was. She patiently worked with Helen, awakening in her a marvelous mind. Against all odds Helen Keller not only learned to write, read Braille, and speak, she graduated cum laude from Radcliffe in 1904 with a Bachelor of Arts degree. She went on to receive numerous awards and accolades.

She struggled against every barrier that stood in her way to reaching her potential. She was enthused about life. Helen once said, "I believe that God is in me as the sun is in the color and fragrance of the flower, the Light in my darkness, the Voice in my silence."

When you get in God, you can get excited about life. One of my favorite quotes from Helen is, "Life is a daring adventure, or nothing."

You have to experiment, risk, and take chances. Someone once said, "Attempt something so big, that if God doesn't show up we are sure to fail." Life is too short to play it safe. You win some; you lose some. "The man who makes no mistakes lacks boldness and the spirit of adventure. He never tries anything new. He is a brake on the wheels of progress," M. W. Larmour said. So what's your excuse?

Life is all about decisions. God has given us the ability to act through the power of choosing. I can pick, choose, or determine what I will do with my life. God has given each of us that free will, that volition, that option, and we had better make wise decisions that won't come back to bite us in the future.

This letter to Ann Landers appeared in newspapers in 1999.

> Dear Ann Landers:
>
> I have been in and out of prison since I was 18 years old, but my problems started long before that.
>
> When I entered junior high school, I began smoking dope, cutting classes and hanging out with the wrong crowd. I drifted along, not making any plans for my future.
>
> For those who are reading this letter, if you are hanging out with a bad crowd, doing drugs, thinking you will get it together eventually — BEWARE.
>
> Steven in Huntsville, Texas, on Death Row

It's about the choices we make today that will determine where we'll be tomorrow. William Jennings Bryan is quoted as saying, "Destiny is not a matter of chance but a matter of choice." Thank God for the power of a choice. We don't have to live foolish, idle, boring lives.

> ## *We can make every minute count by making every choice count.*

I remember watching *The Matrix* in which the main character, Neo, has an incredible epiphany, a moment in which he understands something in a new way through this new manifestation or perception. He discovers that there is more to his life than what he is currently experiencing. He meets Morpheus, who confirms Neo's suspicions about a parallel existence that seems so close he can almost taste it.

During their face-to-face encounter, Morpheus presents an intriguing opportunity for Neo to leave his ordinary but unfulfilling life and venture into the unfamiliar world of the Matrix to learn "the truth" about life. Neo must choose between a blue pill and a red pill, which represents the critical choice that Neo has to make concerning what he wants to do with the rest of his life. The blue pill will allow him to return home to what he had always known, while the red pill will open the door for him to see what the Matrix is truly all about. Morpheus's final statement to Neo in that scene is, "Remember . . . all I'm offering is the truth. Nothing more."

Life is not a science-fiction movie. Life is a quest, an expedition into a world of discovery and destiny. God presents us with choices: blessings or curses, life or death. Now we must choose. "I call heaven and earth as witnesses today against you, that I have set before you life and death, blessing and cursing; therefore choose life, that both you and your descendants may live" (Deut. 30:19).

Choose life!

Thank God for the power of a choice. We don't have to live foolish, idle, boring lives. George Bernard Shaw said, "We are made wise not by the recollection of our past, but by the responsibility for our future."

I like what Phil Cooke said: "Your daily decisions determine your destiny." The question is, what are you doing daily to develop your potential and set the course for your destiny? What are you reading, writing, planning, learning, and praying? Who are you hanging with?

Here are some ways you can develop your potential.

- Pray and seek God's wisdom for your potential.
- Network with other driven leaders.
- Read good books on personal and spiritual growth.
- Know your personality type. Consider Myers-Briggs, the DISC Profile, or Tom Rath's *Strengths Finder*.
- Consider taking a course on leadership development. Consider John Maxwell or Les Brown seminars.
- Visit parks, museums, libraries, neighborhood attractions, as well as your own backyard.

Develop a burning desire to tap into all your potential. Potential comes from the root word *potent* and refers to all the things you can be successful at if you develop and use your gifts, talents, and natural abilities.

Once you know your potential, start developing it. It's a tragedy to waste your potential. Make up your mind right now that you will be a lifelong learner, because the more you learn, the more you earn.

Once you discover your potential, you won't have to guess about it, you can move on it.

Takeaway Points

There's more God-given potential that you and I have not yet tapped into.

You are pregnant with possibilities and potential.

It's a tragedy to waste your potential.

Life is all about decisions.

Questions to Reflect On

What can I be great at?

What do I excel at?

What kind of life do I want to manifest?

What steps can I take today to develop my untapped potential?

9

The Will to Prepare

It's better to look ahead and prepare than to look back and regret.
— Jackie Joyner-Kersee

The Law of Readiness, developed by Edward Thorndike, implies that some opportunities you must simply be ready for and mature enough to handle. You can do many things to prepare to become all you were meant to be: read books, attend conferences, watch Webinars, listen to audio presentations, take notes, journal, learn from those who are where you want to be, adopt a personal life coach and a personal trainer.

Ask yourself these important questions about your life:

3 Stages of Me

How was my life?
How is my present life?
How do I hope my life to be in the future?

Once you understand where you've been and where you are, you will be able to better navigate where you hope to be. Your success or productive living doesn't happen without preparation. Often when we see people who are successful, we fail to see the years of preparation behind the scenes. Many people do not understand that most successful people failed several times along the way.

If you are a person of faith reading this book, you just can't sit back and say, "I have faith," and expect some magical experience to change your life. I believe God will make a way through you and me planning our lives. "Faith without works is dead" (James 2:20).

God is waiting on you to join Him to maximize your life.

Remember that you cannot grow until you first create the capacity for growth. You must be intentional and willing to push yourself. I can push you and encourage you through this book, your teacher can push you, your coach can push you, your parents can push you, your pastor can push you, but until you push yourself, nothing will propel you to progress. That's one reason why I don't believe in New Year's Resolutions; rather, I believe in New Year's Intentions.

Just because you recite a New Year's resolution doesn't guarantee things are going to change. Things change because you intentionally implement a plan of action. You must be intentionally becoming with a plan of action.

Most of us have that drive, that longing, that craving, that inclination to be more than what we are and to reach our fullest potential, but it's only when we take that first step that we are in motion to become our best.

You cannot grow until you first create the capacity for growth.

Your first step of preparation may be reading this book or getting off the couch or writing down five things you want to accomplish in the next five years. Maybe your first step is registering for that college course you've been putting off for the last ten years, recording a single demo, getting back into the gym, or writing that business plan for that business you've wanted to start. The hardest step is the first step, so do it now and get it behind you.

Dare to prepare.

I hated taking tests in school. I didn't study thoroughly for the test mainly because I didn't have study skills, I wasn't part of a study group, and I didn't have the discipline to study. Because of my lack of preparation for the test, I would tremble with fear on test days. I had no confidence, and I felt lost among my peers. I even had the nerve to pray and ask God to bail me out. Some of my best prayers I've prayed were right before I took a test. "Pray like it all depends on God, and work like it all depends on you," Mark Batterson said. I had the praying down but not the working and preparation. Looking back, I think how insane that was not to study for a test. I did not prepare because I did not take school seriously.

Preparation + Opportunity = Destiny

Life is similar to school: if you don't prepare and take it seriously, you can fail tremendously throughout it.

So start preparing for life. It will require training, discipline, and lots of practice. My son plays a trumpet, and he practices rigorously. When he performs, you can hear his preparation in his performance. Once he had to play in New York City and the applause from the crowd and the other band members were very complimentary because his performance was excellent. His practicing also got him accepted into the New School of Jazz on a partial scholarship.

I've learned some lessons on life's journey, and one of those important lessons is there's no bypass to your destiny. The only course of action is to dare to prepare through prayer. George Washington Carver was right when he said, "There is no shortcut to achievement." There's a brutal but true saying about taking the elevator to success: "There is no elevator to success. You have to take the stairs."

Rory Vaden, in his book, *Take the Stairs*, wrote:

> The last time you came up to a set of stairs and an escalator, did you *Take the Stairs*? If you're like 95% of the world, then you probably didn't. Most people don't; most of the time we look for shortcuts. We all want to be successful and we all want to have a happy life, but we constantly look for the easy way. We look for the "escalator" in hopes that life will be easier. Unfortunately, in our search for making things easier, we are actually making them worse.[1]

Taking the stairs requires more work, more sweat, more effort, and more time, but in the end you will be more rewarded for the process and the path you took to get there.

Don't focus on the process; focus on the results.

The difference between winners and losers is preparation. The difference between victory and defeat is preparation.

Abraham Lincoln said, "I will prepare myself, and someday my chance will come." He did prepare himself and when presented with the opportunity to become president of the United States, he took it. Had he not prepared himself, the opportunity would not have come knocking.

Many opportunities never come our way simply because we're not prepared. We try to experience next-level opportunities when we're still living on a lower level. It's like trying to experience a deep life in shallow waters. To experience next-level opportunities, you must prepare to go to the next level.

There are many open doors but maybe not on the level you are on. Some open doors require you to step up to the next level.

Many people are like the Tin Man in *The Wonderful Wizard of Oz*: they rust.

Richard Leider and Stephen Buchholz wrote in their article "The Rustout Syndrome":

> Rustout is the slow death that follows when we stop making choices that keep life alive. It's the feeling of numbness that comes from taking the safe way, never accepting new challenges, continually surrendering to the day-to-day routine. Rustout means we are no longer growing, but at best, are simply maintaining. It implies that we have traded the sensation of life for the security of a paycheck. Rustout is the opposite of burnout. Burnout is overdoing. Rustout is underbeing.[2]

When we stop growing, learning, and improving in our totality, we begin to rust. Oftentimes we are stuck in a routine, in our everyday pattern of sameness. In other words, we stop becoming more. Maya Angelou wrote, "Because of our routines, we forget that life is an ongoing adventure." It's time to break your routine and get your spontaneity back. This is your one and only life. You only get one time around to make it count.

There are only so many tomorrows but many right nows. Start right now.

Prepare right now for your life mission. Be willing to work hard, pray, and sacrifice until you get to the next level. "If the people knew how hard I had to work to gain my mastery, it wouldn't seem wonderful at all," Michelangelo wrote.

Abraham Lincoln once said, "If I had eight hours to chop down a tree, I'd spend six sharpening my axe." Before Abraham Lincoln became the president, he chopped wood for a penny a day. It was the chopping of trees that prepared him for the presidency.

Paul "Bear" Bryant said, "It's not the will to win that matters—everyone has that. It's the will to prepare to win that matters."

When Noah built the ark, it wasn't raining. But when the rain came, he was prepared.

To become the Olympic champion in the gymnastics individual all-around event, Gabby Douglas first had to leave everything she loved. She had to leave her home and family in Virginia Beach. She had to leave her two dogs that were her constant companions. She had to go to Iowa to train to prepare herself for the next level.

She became the first African American to win the all-around Olympic gold in gymnastics. She said, "Gold medals are made of your blood, sweat, and tears in the gym." Her preparation paid off.

Action plans are plans with action.

Before she was the Martha Stewart we know now, she started a catering business in her basement with a friend. Martha continually reached for the next level, which led to her creating cookbooks, decorating tips, and more. Now we know her as a billionaire and founder of Martha Stewart Living. It all began with many years of preparation. Preparation will determine if we are ready for the opportunities. Daily we are preparing for something: either winning or failing. Doing nothing still prepares us—to fail.

Be Prepared by Thinking Ahead

Preparation can be difficult. It can be long and it can be lonely. But when you prepare, God can and will use you. He's given you a dream of making a difference.

You see it happen sometimes: people come across a great opportunity that they're not prepared for. Sometimes you see it at the Oscars when actors win who clearly never dreamed in a million years they would win. As they accept their award, it's obvious they hadn't prepared an acceptance speech.

This happened to Sally Field when she won her Oscar for *Places in the Heart*. All she could think of to say in her acceptance speech was, "You like me. Right now you like me!" William Matthews said, "Unless a man has trained himself for his chance, the chance will only make him look ridiculous." Thankfully, Sally didn't look horribly ridiculous, but she has been teased for years about her "speech."

Abraham Lincoln said, "Without God I cannot succeed. With God I cannot fail." God expects us to do all the necessary preparation to be victorious in our endeavors. Just as the soldier had to train his horse and provide nourishment to the animal, so we need to provide mental and spiritual food for our minds and souls if we expect to be prepared for the battles of life. General MacArthur said, "The most important lesson I learned at West Point is preparation is one key to victory." It is always better to be over-prepared than under-prepared for your tasks.

Before I became an author, I had to prepare writing this manuscript in several states across America. Writing *The Will to Be* took over a year. As I wrote it, I had to prepare myself to self-publish and market the book while still building my platform. I had to find well-respected endorsers with credibility and influence. I had to pay for the publishing services, pay the editor for editing and proofreading, find a graphic designer to design the front and back covers, find a company to make it available on Audible.com—all of this preparation took place before my book ever made it on Amazon, iBooks, and Barnes & Noble. Had I not made all those preparations, you would not be holding this book in your hands.

Takeaway Points

You cannot grow until you first create the capacity for growth.

The difference between victory and defeat is preparation.

Life is similar to school: if you don't prepare and take it seriously, you can fail tremendously throughout it.

This is your one and only life. You get only one time around to make it count.

Questions to Reflect On

Why is preparation so important?
How are you preparing for your next level of growth?
Are you willing to take the stairs?
How will you make your one and only life count?

10

The Will to Believe

More people fail from a lack of faith than from of talent.
—Billy Sunday

Many people never become more than what they are because they don't believe they can. When you have a defeated mind-set like the ten spies in the Old Testament story of Moses and the Israelites trying to possess the Promised Land, there's no way you can win.

Here's the story in brief. Moses sent twelve men to investigate the land God promised to give to His people, the Israelites. The twelve men returned after a forty-day excursion, and ten of the men feared they couldn't take the land because of the giants they saw there. Two of the men trusted God and believed they could take possession of the land. One of those men, Caleb, gave this report to the Israelite community:

> "Let's go at once to take the land," he said. "We can certainly conquer it!"

But the other men who had explored the land with him disagreed. "We can't go up against them! They are stronger than we are!"

So they spread this bad report about the land among the Israelites: "The land we traveled through and explored will devour anyone who goes to live there. All the people we saw were huge. We even saw giants there, the descendants of Anak. Next to them we felt like grasshoppers, and that's what they thought, too!" (Num. 13:30–33)

Caleb spoke faith talk—claiming victory before the battle. I believe you must have heart faith and say-it faith.

Unfortunately, the people listened to the ten spies rather than to Caleb. As a result, the people spent the next forty years in the wilderness and forfeited their destiny because of some giants. When you're trying to get to your destiny, you will see God and giants, but you must choose to stay focused on God.

Because of a lack of faith, the Israelites developed the following:

- grasshopper mentality
- inferiority complex
- low self-esteem
- analysis paralysis
- fear of failure

They were on the edge of greatness, at the intersection of possibilities and opportunities, only days away from the Promised Land, yet they let fear rule the day and paid for that mistake the rest of their lives. If you are reading this book, you could be closer to your promised land than you think. Or maybe you're only a few months or perhaps years away from your destiny of becoming more. Yet you may find yourself at a crisis of belief. Make today the day you decide whether to press on to greatness or retreat to a wilderness of mediocrity. Between today and your tomorrow is always a faith test. Corrie Ten Boom wrote, "Faith sees the invisible, believes the unbelievable, and receives the impossible."

Faith keeps the person who keeps the faith.

When life interferes, and trust me it will, you must rely on your faith. When your dreams are delayed, and trust me they will be, rely on your faith. When you have a setback, and trust me you will, you must rely on your faith. Life sometimes will bring the unexpected, the unthinkable, even the unimaginable. That's when you rely on your faith. William Newton Clarke said, "Faith is the daring of the soul to go farther than it can see."

Faith is one of the most powerful gifts we possess.

Years ago I heard a powerful song on faith that defined what faith can accomplish. Vanessa Bell Armstrong's song "Faith" says:

Faith to reach the unreachable,
faith to fight the unbeatable,
faith to remove the unmovable,
faith that stands the invincible,
faith that can conquer anything.
I believe that faith can conquer anything.

Faith can move mountains just as the Bible says. We can read countless stories of people who had faith to see their bodies healed, circumstances changed, and lives enriched. No matter what your circumstances, believe, keep believing, and believe some more.

When your critics say you won't amount to anything, keep believing you will. When you get a negative doctor's report, keep believing you will be healed and that your body will get stronger. When you are passed over for the promotion, keep believing that your hard work and dedication will not be forgotten. When the bank disapproves your loan, keep believing that there's one bank that will approve the loan you need. When your book manuscript is rejected, keep believing that a publishing company will pick it up. If you are in poverty, believe you will come out to a life of prosperity.

When you lose faith and stop believing, something inside you starts to die: your dreams, your hopes, your potential, and your future. I grew up in a tough community where many people lost the faith because their dreams and visions were broken and shattered; because of their lack of faith, many fell through the cracks of life, so to speak. So instead of believing again, many people just stop believing and settle far short of what God had planned for their lives. I dare you to live by faith; I dare you to believe by faith; and I dare you to expect in faith.

Either we are living by faith, or we're not living at all.

Faith is risky at times, and sometimes it's dangerous. I believe in the old saying, "The greater the risk, the greater the reward." Living by faith is living that pleases God, who wants you to see the dreams He has placed in your heart come to pass. I have so many dreams and visions inside me that no one knows except God, my wife, and me. Faith is seeing what others can't see. Although your dreams may seem far away, in reality they are as close to you as your heart.

I love the story that John Magliola tells of the small boy and the star. "A small boy looked at a star and began to weep. The star said, 'Boy, why are you weeping?' And the boy said, 'You are so far away. I will never be able to touch you.' And the star answered, 'Boy, if I were not already in your heart, you would not be able to see me.'"[1]

Now that you know your dreams are closer than you thought, you can almost reach up by faith and touch them. Dr. Martin Luther King Jr. said, "Faith is taking the first step in faith. You don't have to see the whole staircase. Just take the step." Faith is an action word. It makes you move forward; it makes you write out plans and goals. It makes you fill out applications for employment. It makes you enroll in a university without knowing how you will get tuition. It makes you write the business plan without any funding for your business. Faith makes you write a book without a publisher. Always believe. Never let the naysayers and doubters cause you to lose faith.

---

*Let people doubt you, and let
God prove them wrong.*

I had to believe in my dreams as though I was holding on to a wing and a prayer. I had an anchor in the principles of the Bible, which kept me believing and optimistic. When I planted the ministry Above & Beyond Fellowship, where I serve as Senior Pastor, it took us eighteen years to purchase land and twenty-one years to start building the campus. At all eight of our different locations throughout the years, I had to keep believing that God would bless us to build a permanent multimillion-dollar church home. When my wife was diagnosed with leukemia, I had to keep believing through all eight rounds of chemo treatments at Houston's

M. D. Anderson Hospital that God would heal her. While living in apartments for ten-and-a-half years of our marriage, I had to believe that God would honor our faith by allowing us to purchase a brand-new home. While attending six different colleges over eighteen years, I had to keep believing that one day I would earn my Bachelor's Degree. While writing this book, I had to believe that I would get favorable endorsements. Although I experienced too many other tests to mention here, through each one of them I was positive, optimistic, and always believing.

What has been your story when you wanted to give up? I say to you, put on your faith face and believe again. Believe that someday you will have a dream career; believe that someday you will marry your soul mate; believe that someday you will give birth to a child; believe that someday you will be free from addictions; believe that someday you will be debt free; believe that someday you will travel the world. Believe and keep on believing. Don't give up, look up. It was David's belief that kept him from giving up. "I would have lost heart, unless I had believed that I would see the goodness of the Lord in the land of the living" (Ps. 27:13).

Claude Bristol wrote:

> Gradually I discovered that there is a golden thread that runs through all the teachings and makes them work for those who sincerely accept and apply them, and that thread can be named in a single word— belief. It is the same element, belief, which causes people to be healed, enables others to climb high the ladder of success, and gets phenomenal results for all who accept it.... have no doubt about it, there is something magical in believing.[2]

The Will To Be

There's something supernatural about believing. My favorite song from the soundtrack to *The Prince of Egypt*, a great animated movie inspired by the biblical story of the Israelites' exodus from Egypt, was written by Stephen Schwartz and Kenneth (Baby Face) Edmonds titled "When You Believe." A couple of lines from the bridge stand out: "There can be miracles when you believe" and "Who knows what miracles you can achieve when you believe."

Your dreams, your visions are possible through faith. Anybody can give up when times are rough and challenging, but a person of faith believes that where there is a will, God will make a way. Be careful not to talk yourself out of your dream possibilities. Daniel Amen, psychiatrist and neuroscientist said, "Don't believe everything you hear, even in your own mind." Don't listen to the voice of self-doubt; only listen to the optimistic voice of faith.

It reminds me of the story of the two frogs that fell into the cream.

Two frogs fell into a deep cream bowl,
One was an optimistic soul.
But the other took a gloomy view,
"I shall drown!" he cried "and so will you!"
So with a last despairing cry,
He closed his eyes and said good-bye!
But the other with a merry grin said,
"I can't get out, but I won't give in!
I'll swim around until my strength is spent,
For having tried I'll die content."
Bravely, he swam until it would seem,
His struggles began to churn the cream.
On top of the butter at last he stopped,
And out of the bowl he happily hopped.

What is the moral? It's easily found: keep swimming, keep believing like the optimistic frog and some way, somehow, God will see you through. "Jesus said to him, 'If you can believe, all things are possible to him who believes'" (Mark 9:23).

Takeaway Points

The easiest thing to do is to give up.
There's something supernatural about believing.
Faith is seeing what others can't see.
Faith is an action word.

Questions to Reflect On

Do you live with doubt?
Have negative people ever told you to give up?
Why is it so hard to keep believing?
What will you do to become more optimistic?

11

The Will to Make a Comeback

Failure is the only opportunity to begin again more intelligently.
—Henry Ford

H ave you ever felt like a failure? If you answer yes, I can relate. I'm so familiar with failure that I have earned the right to write the chapter about it. I've learned so much through failing, and one of the biggest lessons I've learned is that after failing you can make a comeback. It's never too late to rebuild and rebound from failure. It's never too late to make a comeback. It's never too late to recover. It's never too late to improve. It's never too late to do better and be better. It's never too late to resurface.

The key to overcoming failure is to learn from it, grow from it, and move past it.

In his book *Maximize the Moment: God's Action Plan for Your Life,*" T. D. Jakes wrote the following about a place called "there":

> It doesn't matter where "there" is for you. It matters that you achieve soul satisfaction. It matters that you reach your full purpose and potential. It matters that you attain your highest and best use. If you sense as you read this that you're not "there," that's okay. There is no harm in not being "there" if you are on your way, you're in hot pursuit, in the process of journeying to a place called "there." The real tragedy is when you're not even going in the right direction. It means you're lost. It means you've lost. It means you have spent many days, months, or even years, which you cannot reclaim, and you haven't even begun the real journey. But the good news is that if you realize that you have been running in circles, you can stop and make today, right now, a starting place. Every journey must start somewhere, and the time is now if you are not already on your way. Remember that setbacks are really setups for you to come forward and reassess where you are and where you are going.[1]

I began failing ninth and tenth grades because my learning skills were weak. So I enrolled in my first summer school class, only to fail. I entered the eleventh grade, but I had to attend night school to make up the classes I failed in ninth and tenth grades. I had to accept the fact that I would not graduate with my original class, the class of '84.

I still wanted to attend that graduation, so without permission, on Saturday, May 26, 1984, at 5:00 pm, I showed up at the "Booker T. Washington Senior High School and High School for Engineering Professions Commencement located at the Music Hall in downtown Houston, Texas. I had to see it, witness it, and experience the graduation that should have been mine. As they began to call the students' names from the class of '84, I was familiar with many of them, for some of the students I had played street basketball and football with. Some of us rode bikes together and fought together. Some of us took classes together in middle and high school. This graduation was a very emotional time for me, because when they started calling the names of the students whose last names began with the letter *L*, I started thinking they would call my name right about now.

At this point a lot of serious emotions and thoughts ran through my mind: regret, wondering how I got so far behind, and feeling like a failure. Honestly, I ached; I hurt. Benjamin Franklin was right when he said, "The things which hurt, instruct." The toughest moment was when I heard the name *William Linne* announced (how close is that to William Lindsey?), yet at the same time it was an encouraging moment. Tough because I should have been on that stage with a cap and gown, moving my tassel from left to right; and encouraging because I promised myself, "Next year I will be on that stage, hearing my name called, and graduating with the class of '85. I will make a comeback next year. I'm God's child and I have a will to make a comeback."

Let's fast-forward this story 357 days. One year later, same month, same place, same time: Saturday, May 18, 1985. As they called my name, I walked across that stage with boldness, confidence and praise, joy and excitement. I did not let failure define my life. I did not let one failure become the narrative of my whole life story. I changed my attitude, became disciplined, and became the comeback kid.

---

*Do not let failure become the
narrative of your life story.*

 ## William J. Lindsey

I'm sure you're familiar with "If at first you don't succeed, try, try again." If you try again, you will be a comeback kid too. Willie Jolley, in his book *A Setback Is a Setup for a Comeback*, wrote, "In every life there comes a time, a minute when you must decide to stand up and live your dreams or fall back and live your fears. In that minute of decision, you must grasp the vision and seize the power that lies deep inside of you. Then you will see that dreams really can and do come true and that all things truly are possible . . . If you can just believe!"

Shortly after graduating high school, I attended the University of Houston, only to reunite myself with failure. Yes, I failed tremendously. I had no study skills and was by no means disciplined. I found comfort in hanging out in the halls rather than taking my education seriously. I returned the next year to U of H, only to fail again. Two years later, in 1988, I attended Houston Community College and proceeded to flunk. I failed my third attempt at college. Although I was failing repeatedly, I never viewed failure as a permanent defeat, but rather as a temporary fall. William D. Brown was right when he said, "Failure is an event, never a person."

In 1990, I went for my fourth attempt, returning to Houston Community College. I received my first six college credits, which helped build momentum to keep pressing toward my first college degree, which took about another thirteen years to complete. Now with a Bachelor's Degree, Master's Degree, and recently accepted into a university as future Doctoral Candidate, I've learned that the race is not given to the swift nor to the strong but to the one who endures to the end.

For example, look at the life of Abraham Lincoln; he's a man who was familiar with failure.

He failed in business, age 22

He ran for legislature, defeated, age 23

He again failed in business, age 24

The Will To Be

He was elected to legislature, age 25
His sweetheart died, age 26
His dad had a nervous breakdown, age 27
He was defeated for Speaker, age 29
He was defeated for Elector, age 31
He was defeated for Congress, age 34
He was elected to Congress, age 37
He was defeated for Congress, age 39
He was defeated for Senate, age 46
He was defeated for vice president, age 47
He was defeated for Senate, age 49
He was elected president of the United States, age 51

He had many more sorrows, yet Abraham Lincoln refused to let his failures define him and fought significant odds to achieve greatness.

Just because you failed doesn't mean you're a failure. Never let failure defeat you or define you.

Thomas Edison estimated that he failed at making the light bulb 10,000 times and was proud of it. After he finally invented a workable light bulb, he said that if this try had failed, he'd still be trying other ways to make it work.

I stumbled upon this poem about failure:

Failure does not mean—I'm a failure;
It does mean I have not yet succeeded.
Failure does not mean I have accomplished nothing;
It does mean I have learned something.
Failure does not mean I have been a fool;
It does mean I had enough faith to experiment.
Failure does not mean I have disgraced;
It does mean I have dared to try.
Failure does not mean I don't have it;

It does mean I have something to do in a different way.
Failure does not mean I am inferior;
It does mean I am not perfect.
Failure does not mean I have wasted my life;
It does mean that I have an excuse to start over.
Failure does not mean that I should give up;
It does mean that I should try harder.
Failure does not mean that I will never make it;
It does mean that I need more practice.
Failure does not mean that God has abandoned me;
It does mean that God has a better way for you.

(Author unknown)

If you're not failing, you're not learning. Failure can cause one to reevaluate his life, to consider again, especially with the possibility of change or reversing his strategy. Failure should cause a person to reevaluate, reexamine, and rethink her life.

Michael Jordan, arguably the greatest NBA basketball player, stated, "I have missed more than 9,000 shots in my career. I have lost almost 300 games. On twenty-six occasions, I have been entrusted to take the game winning shot, and I missed. I have failed over and over and over again in my life. And that is why I succeed."

When you think of Steve Jobs, you think of innovation, creativity, and genius; you think of iPod, MacBooks, iTunes, iPhone, iPad, and so on. He transformed technology. Yet Steve Jobs was a serial failure.

Back in the pre-floppy-disk days, many people considered the Apple I and Apple II computers failures. A personal computer named Lisa never really took off the ground, the Macintosh computers never panned out, which put Jobs out of a job. Of course, now we know that Jobs didn't give up.

He turned his failures into a huge success that has changed technology in the twenty-first century.

Walt Disney is another example of a person who failed before becoming successful. A newspaper editor fired Disney because "he lacked imagination and had no good ideas." He went bankrupt several times before he built Disneyland. In fact, the city of Anaheim rejected Disney's proposed park on the grounds that it would only attract trash. He became one of the greatest dreamers of our time; he created the first sound cartoon, the first all-color cartoon, and the first animated feature-length motion picture. He showed us that after a failure, you can make a comeback. Today we have The Walt Disney Company, a global enterprise:

- Disneyland Resort
- Walt Disney World Resort
- Tokyo Disney Resort
- Disneyland Paris
- Hong Kong Disneyland Resort
- Shanghai Disney Resort
- Disney Cruise Line
- Disney Vacation Club
- Adventures by Disney
- Disney Regional Entertainment
- Walt Disney Imagineering
- Walt Disney Creative Entertainment
- The Disney Channel

You get it, Disney everything.

The race is not given to the swift or to the strong but to the one who endures to the end.

If you have never failed, it's more than likely you have never tried. Just remember that failure is not final unless you give up. I've learned that one can fail forward toward success. As a matter of fact, from my experience, failure is absolutely necessary to succeeding. I'm sure I will fail again, but I will learn to fail better and wiser.

I agree with Dr. William Mayo, who said, "Lord, deliver me from the man who never makes a mistake."

Someone once said, "To win a victory, you must risk a failure." I don't regret failing. It has been through my failures that I have been able to tell others that failure is not the last part of their stories, their movies, or their songs. There is a continuation to your life. In many cases, your best life started where your last failure ended. I believe your best years are ahead of you.

Your next chapter can be your blessed and best chapter.

You have to be perpetual if you are serious about making a comeback. You must have laser-sharp focus, sure determination, and bulldog tenacity.

In November 2001, *Sports Illustrated* ran an article titled "Bouncing Back Big Time," which focused on the Top Ten Greatest Comebacks of All Time:

10. Elvis Presley, 1968—Following years of making schlocky movies, the King wows fans and critics with an electrifying live 1968 TV special, *Elvis* on NBC.

9. Ludwig Wittgenstein, 1929—After quitting academia to teach primary school and to labor as a gardener, he returns to Cambridge University to begin Philosophical Investigations, the seminal work of 20th-century Anglo-American philosophy.

8. Go-go boots, 2000—Three decades after their kicky heyday, the knee-high footwear stages a surprising fashion revival.

7. Harry Truman, 1948—Trailing in the polls by a wide margin for most of the presidential campaign, he turns the Chicago *Tribune*'s DEWEY DEFEATS TRUMAN edition into a future treasure on eBay.

6. Humanity, 14th century—After 25 million Europeans perish, mankind surges back from the Black Death.

5. Muhammad Ali, 1974—Seven years after being stripped of his title and his boxing license, the Greatest KO's George Foreman in Zaire to win back the belt.

4. John Travolta, 1994—Defibrillates his comatose movie career by taking a star turn in *Pulp Fiction*.

3. Michael Jordan, 1995—Quits baseball to make first triumphant comeback.

2. Japan and Germany, 1950s—Former Axis powers rise from the ashes of World War II to become industrial superpowers.

1. Jesus Christ, 33 A.D.—Defies critics and stuns the Romans with his resurrection.

If Jesus made a comeback, you can too. It's not over yet; just remember never to put a period where God has placed a comma. "I can do all things through Christ who gives me the strength" (Phil. 4:13).

Takeaway Points

Never view failure as a permanent defeat, but rather as a temporary fall.

There is a continuation to your life.

Your best life can start where your last failure ended.
It's never too late to make a comeback.

Questions to Reflect On

What have you learned from failure?
How will you respond if you fail again?
In what ways will you fail better?
How will you help others make a comeback from failure?

12

The Will to Hope

Hope is faith on tiptoes.

—William J. Lindsey

aith is believing, but hope is expecting. When you lose hope, you settle for a life of regularity and predictability. You become discontent in your efforts, suicidal in your thinking, and, if you're not careful, you could assassinate your destiny. When you lose hope you may as well call the undertaker. Someone once said, "Man can live about forty days without food, about three days without water, about eight minutes without air, but only one second without hope." It's a tragedy to lose hope. Emil Brunner said, "What oxygen is to the lungs, such is hope to the meaning of life."

Jim Burns tells this story in his book *The Purity Code*:

> Many years ago, a man was traveling across the country by sneaking from one freight train to the next. One night he climbed into what he

thought was a boxcar. He closed the door, which automatically locked shut and trapped him inside. When his eyes adjusted to the light, he realized he was inside a refrigerated boxcar, and he became aware of the intense, freezing cold. He called for help and pounded on the door, but all the noise he made from inside the car failed to attract anyone's attention. After many hours of struggling, he lay down on the floor of the railroad car.

As he tried to fight against the freezing cold, he scratched a message on the floor explaining his unfortunate, imminent death. Late the next day, repairmen from the railroad opened the door and found the dead man inside. Though the man had all the appearance of having frozen to death, the truth was the repairmen had come to fix the broken refrigerator unit in that car. Most likely the temperature of the railroad car had never fallen below fifty degrees during the night. The man had died because he thought he was freezing to death.[1]

Hope will jolt new life into your spirit and rekindle your vision. Inspirational singer and artist India.Arie, in her song "There's Hope," sings about meeting a young man in Brazil, who was poor and blind, "but that didn't keep him from seein' the light . . . he taught me paradise is in your mind."

This young man had no sight, but he had vision. He was in extreme poverty but richer than most people with plenty. Although he was blind and in poverty, he had hope. Dr. Martin Luther King Jr. said, "Everything that is done in the world is done by hope."

It's a tragedy to lose hope.

New York Times best-selling author Dr. Les Parrot wrote in his book *You're Stronger Than You Think*, "Even if we reach our goals to become the success we imagine, we're likely to feel empty. Why emptiness? Because our greatest hope is not fame, comfort, wealth, or power. These are shallow hopes. Our greatest hope is far deeper. Whether we know it or not, our greatest hope is for meaning." I agree. When you have hope, you have significance and you can stand tall and bold, regardless of your circumstances.

Faith believes, but hope expects.

That's what hope does, it won't let you die. Hope will reactivate and revitalize a wind in your soul. When your back is against the wall and the walls of life are caving in on you, hope will make you believe one more time, pray one more time, expect one more time, and wait one more time. You need hope to cope. Cornel West, professor of African American studies at Princeton, said, "We need Hope on a tight rope." Even If the rope of hope breaks, we need to reach beyond the break. Too many people are hopeless and lack expectations; they are despondent with no signs of a favorable outcome. I can tell a hopeless person by looking them in their eyes. You can sense the loss of life and expectancy.

Losing hope can cause illness in the body. Since our hearts, minds, and bodies are interconnected, when one gets infected, it can damage to the other two. "Hope deferred makes the heart sick" (Prov. 13:12). For an example, if we live a healthy lifestyle and perform our spiritual duties, that's good. But if the mind is not healthy, the heart and body cannot make up for the lack, and we are not truly holistically healthy or healed.

Losing hope can cause illness in the body.

In 2012, when my mom was sick, she spent eight days in the hospital. She had hope, I had hope, and my family had hope that she would get better. Mom kept saying, "I'm waiting on the Lord," never complaining but always hoping. She was an amazing woman of hope, always hoping and believing that things will get better.

I recall vividly the last two years of her life when she began to have some serious health challenges. She was so hopeful, never showing signs of giving up, although she was in pain. She always expected the best. Orison Marden said, "There's no medicine like hope, no incentive so great, and no tonic so powerful as expectation of something better tomorrow."

Losing hope is one of the unhealthiest things you can do. Hopelessness can breed greater mental or emotional problems. Death, divorce, job loss, and chronic illness can cause tremendous stress, distress, and feelings of hopelessness in your life.

When I was seventeen, my father had a massive stroke. Doctors pronounced him brain dead. We had very little expectation of a full recovery for my father, because the damage from the stroke was severe. Notice, I didn't say that we didn't have any hope, we had very little hope. We continued to hope, although the outlook did not warrant a recovery. We were hoping against hope for a change in his condition. Regardless of what the doctors said, we hoped against their report. I love what Margaret Weis said, "Hope is the denial of reality."

Although we had faith and hope, our outcome for a full recovery grew dim as complications occurred in my father's body, which led to his passing.

I learned from that experience that it is never over until the last breath leaves your body.

It is never over until God says it's over; until then you must have the courage to hope.

Charles Allen once said, "When you say a situation or a person is hopeless, you are slamming the door in the face of God." No one but God has a right to say a situation is hopeless. Always keep hope and know that God can do the impossible, the unthinkable, and the unimaginable if you believe and hope.

Both of my grandmothers, the late Dorothy Mae Ashley and the late Annie Lindsey, were women of strong faith and hope. My grandmother on my mother's side of the family, Dorothy Mae Ashley, was a former sharecropper. She and her generation made it through one of the toughest times in the history of our country, the Great Depression. My grandmother on my father's side of the famiy, Annie Lindsey, was a praying women whose hope was anchored in God. These two women were warriors in the army of the Lord. Their generation would often say, "God, you have been our help in ages past and you're our hope for years to come." They had a real hope on a firm foundation. Not a counterfeit version of hope, which wants wealth without work and opportunities without sacrificing. They talked about hope, sang about hope, and prayed in hope.

Any level of hope keeps you in the game.

Hope is something that you can't see, but you can truly feel it.

Jean Kerr once said, "Hope is the feeling that the feeling you have isn't permanent." Many times I would have to catch two metro buses to get across town to my job that paid a meager rate, but I never thought it would be my permanent career. I remember working for a company for two years without a raise, but I never felt I would be stuck in that dead-end career. I hoped that someway somehow a change would come.

When you get a jolt of hope, it reenergizes and invigorates your spirit. People with hope look forward with reasonable confidence to the thing they are hopeful for. Many people lose hope and fall back into addictions and defeated mind-sets. Hope is stronger than despair and more daring than gloom. When things look bad, many people begin to despair. In the face of discouragement, our only true hope is in God. The psalmist (the sons of Korah) sang to God by way of asking their souls a question, "'Why are you cast down, O my soul? Why are you disquieted within me?' They answered, 'Hope in God'" (Ps. 43:5).

Victor Hugo wrote, "Hope is the word which God has written on the brow of every man."

Dale Carnegie said, "Most of the important things in the world have been accomplished by people who have kept on trying when there seemed to be no hope at all."

Take, for example, the story of Bethany Hamilton, an American professional surfer. On October 31, 2003, at the age of thirteen, Hamilton went for a morning surf along Tunnels Beach, Kauai. Around 7:30 AM, with numerous turtles in the area, she was lying on her surfboard with her left arm dangling in the water when a fifteen-foot tiger shark attacked her, severing her left arm just below the shoulder. Her friends helped paddle her back to shore then rushed her to Wilcox Memorial Hospital. By the time she arrived, she had lost over 60 percent of her blood. Despite the trauma of the incident, Hamilton determined to return to surfing. She eventually taught herself to surf with one arm and continued to compete.

After only a little more than year after the attack, she took first place in the Explorer Women's division of the 2005 NSSA National Championships. Bethany is an example of a person who learned hope in the midst of adversity. She has become a source of inspiration to millions through her story of faith, determination, and hope.

Bethany said this about hope: "Here's my advice: don't put all your hope and faith into something that could suddenly and easily disappear. And honestly, that's almost anything. The only thing that will never go away, that will never fail you, is God and your faith in him." If you have the will to hope, and put your hope and faith in God, you can expect and anticipate a favorable future. Remember that faith is the substance of things hoped for. (See Hebrews 11:19.)

Takeaway Points

Faith believes; hope expects.
Any level of hope keeps you in the game.
When you lose hope you may as well call the undertaker.
You need hope to cope.

Questions to Reflect On

Why is hope so important?
What happens when a person loses hope?
What does hope do to the body?
How hopeful are you about your future?

13

The Will to Face
Your Fears

Fear is that little darkroom where negatives are developed.
—Michael Pritchard

"Fear not" appears over 300 hundred times in the Bible.

According to the National Institute of Mental Health, approximately 50 million American adults are diagnosed with anxiety disorder. Anxiety is called the epidemic of the twenty-first century. Behavioral psychologists say that the only fears we are born with are the fear of falling and the fear of loud noises. All other fears are learned, and like a bad habit, they can be unlearned.

Ed Young Jr. said, "Fear is an unavoidable part of the human experience." Instead of avoiding our fears, we should face our fears. David was a fear facer when he confronted the undefeated giant named Goliath. Peter was a fear facer when he attempted to walk on water. Queen Esther was a fear facer when she said, "If I perish, I perish." If you struggle with a certain fear, serve notice that you can't fix what you won't face. Learn to face what you fear.

The following are the top ten fears most people have.

1. Fear of flying
2. Fear of public speaking
3. Fear of heights
4. Fear of the dark
5. Fear of intimacy
6. Fear of death
7. Fear of failure
8. Fear of rejection
9. Fear of spiders
10. Fear of commitment

According to the *American Heritage Dictionary*, fear is "an emotion of alarm and agitation caused by the expectation or realization of danger."

"A four-year-old child had a bad experience with a local anesthetic for stitches taken from her forehead. When she went to the dentist to have some baby teeth extracted, she screamed hysterically in the dentist's chair. He gave the child a sedative to quiet her for the examination. Within a few minutes after having her teeth removed, the child had a heart attack and was rushed to the hospital where she died two days later. The autopsy found very high levels of adrenaline in her blood stream due to fear that caused her to have a heart attack. Fear of the dentist resulted in the child's death. So we see that excess fear can be catastrophic on a man's mind."[1]

Many people live in fear of fear. Often Jesus would tell His followers, "Oh, you have little faith." Notice, He never said, "Oh, you with big fears." He always stressed faith, not fear.

Fear is negative and faith is positive. Fear paralyzes, while faith mobilizes. Napoleon said, "He who fears being conquered is sure of defeat."

Once you let fear conquer your will and your mind, you will neither face nor fix the things you need to confront.

Maybe fear has told you that you could never start a business, go back to school, or apologize to the person who hurt you. Maybe fear has told you that you could never be a public speaker or be committed to a relationship because of broken trust in the past. Do me one favor, stop listening to the voice of fear. The more you listen to the voice of fear, the more negative you become. Many people never develop to their full potential because of fear.

The parable in Matthew 25:14–30 tells of a master who was leaving his home to travel. Before leaving, he entrusted his property to his servants. One servant received five talents, the second received two talents, and the third one talent, according to their respective abilities.

Returning after a long absence, the master called in his servants and asked them for an accounting. The first two servants explained that they had each put the money to work and doubled the value of the property. The master rewarded them.

The third servant, however, had hidden his talent in a hole in the ground. The master punished him. The reason the servant hid his talent? "I was afraid and went and hid your talent in the ground" (Matt. 25:25).

Fear will hold you back from trying, from daring, from risking. Fear will cause you to live as a cowardly lion instead of a brave heart. Fear will cause you to put off for tomorrow the things you need to do today. Fear will cause you to make excuses for not moving forward. Fear will cripple your will to become more. Fear always paralyzes and weakens willpower.

As a leader, I have to model bravery, for no one really wants to follow a weak, timid leader. William Wallace said, "People follow courage, not titles." God told Joshua to be courageous four times in Joshua chapter 1.

Fear will keep you on the sidelines of life.

Fear will cause you to falter, flinch, and cringe. Fear will keep you frozen in a time period from which you should have graduated. Fear will keep you in an unhealthy, abusive, and dysfunctional relationship you know is not safe. Fear will keep you from going to the doctor when you have pain in your body. Fear will destroy your faith and keep you living a shallow life.

Bruce Wilkinson wrote in *The Dream Giver*:

> Still trembling, Ordinary picked up his suitcase, turned his back on Familiar, and walked to the sign. And even though his fear kept growing, he shut his eyes and took a big step forward—right through the invisible Wall of Fear.
>
> And there he made a surprising discovery. On the other side of that single step—the exact one Ordinary didn't think he could take—he found that he had broken through his Comfort Zone.[2]

If you face your fears, you will discover that you enlarged and magnified the thing you feared. "Worry gives a small thing a big shadow" (old Swedish Proverb).

Another common fear is what we think other people say about us. The truth is people are going to talk about you whether you do good or bad, so you may as well continue doing good, being productive, and advancing your life. Instead of worrying about what people think, live in such a way that you give them something to talk about. You were never made to please people, so don't try now. Abraham Lincoln said, "You can please some of the people some of the time, all of the people some of the time, some of the people all of the time, but you can never please all of the people all of the time." Trying to please people will zap you of your energy. Besides, you will never make everyone happy, so take that energy and strive to be productive. Another way I like to put it is learn to live for an audience of One.

> *You have no control over what people say or think about you, so stop trying to defend yourself and focus on pleasing God and fulfilling your purpose.*

Remember, in this chapter you want to focus on the word *faith*. If you are going to overcome fear, you must listen to the voice of faith, because the voice of faith is always hopeful and opportunistic. Billy Sunday said, "Fear knocked at my door. Faith answered, and there was no one there." Faith always attacks fear and leads you to do the impossible. So feed your faith, then watch your fears starve to death.

One fear many people need to overcome is the fear to take a stand in the midst of injustice. Dr. Martin Luther King Jr. said:

> You may be thirty-eight years old, as I happen to be. And one day, some great opportunity stands before you and calls you to stand up for some great principle, some great issue, some great cause. And you refuse to do it because you are afraid.... You

129

refuse to do it because you want to live longer....
You're afraid that you will lose your job, or you are
afraid that you will be criticized or that you will
lose your popularity or you're afraid that somebody
will stab you or shoot at you or bomb your house;
so you refuse to take the stand. Well, you may go on
and live until you are ninety, but you're just as dead
at thirty-eight as you would be at ninety. And the
cessation of breathing in your life is but the belated
announcement of an earlier death of the spirit.

Never allow fear to keep you silent when you see injustices;
always do the right thing, even if it costs you your job, your
friends, and your popularity.

Never make a decision based on fear. "For God has not
given us a spirit of fear, but of power and of love and of a sound
mind" (2 Tim. 1:7).

Denis Waitley said, "Procrastination is the fear of success.
People procrastinate because they are afraid of the success that
they know will result if they move ahead now. Because success
is heavy, carries a responsibility with it, it is much easier to
procrastinate and live on the 'someday I'll' philosophy."

Paul Wilson Jr., in his book on dreams titled *Dream Big in
3D,* talks about the movie of *Akeelah and the Bee.*

The main character, an extremely bright young
girl name Akeelah, is being coached to compete at
the national spelling bee by a college professor and
former spelling bee participant. However, prior to
agreeing to be tutored, she had rejected his offer.
She did not initially want to be tutored, because
she thought she could do it on her own. She was
naturally talented, but she had never really pushed
herself beyond her comfort zone. She finally decided
that she didn't want to be just a good speller, she

wanted to be a great one. So it was at this point in the movie when the professor asked Akeelah to read a poem that he had on the wall of his office, which was "Our Deepest Fear" by Marianne Williamson. The poem is incredibly inspiring and empowering. In it Williams challenges us as human beings to not be afraid of ourselves—the wonderfully unique and phenomenally potent individuals that God has created us to be."[3]

You are a child of God. Playing small does not serve the world. There's nothing enlightened about shrinking so that other people won't feel insecure around you. We were born manifesting the glory of God that is within us. God has created us in His image to be bold, courageous and fearless. Like many people in life, Akeelah was intimidated by fear, mainly the fear to succeed, because she could not handle her God-given strengths and gifts. Remember to believe what God says about you. Remember to face your fears.

Growing up in the '70s, my siblings and I loved to watch our favorite cartoons. Mine was *Underdog*. The Shoeshine Boy's heroic alter ego appeared whenever love interest, Sweet Polly Purebred, was being victimized by such villains as Simon Bar Sinister or Riff Raff. When villains threatened Sweet Polly, she sang in a somewhat whining tone, "Oh where, oh where has my Underdog gone?"

Once Underdog got wind of her troubling voice, Shoeshine Boy would duck into a telephone booth where he transformed into the caped and costumed hero, destroying the booth in the process when his super powers were activated. Underdog would come out speaking in rhyme. One of the rhymes was, "I am not slow, For it's hip-hip-hip and AWAY I GO!"

When he showed up on the scene to capture the villains and rescue Polly, he would say his most famous rhyme, "There's no need to fear; Underdog is here!"[4]

Here's the point: you're not Underdog, you are a Top Dog, and you don't need a telephone booth to get the willpower, strength, and faith you need to face and conquer your fears. You have a prayer closet. When we overcome our fears, we become champions of faith.

Takeaway Points

Learn to face what you fear.
Fear will cause you not to try, not to dare, and not to risk.
Faith always attacks fear and leads you to do the impossible.
You were never made to please people, so don't try now.

Questions to Reflect On

What has been one of your biggest fears?
How have you conquered your biggest fear?
Does it bother you what other people think of you?
Does fear keep you silent when you see injustice?

14

The Will to Forgive

Holding a grudge is letting someone live rent free in your head.
—Unknown

All our lives we have heard that two things are certain: death and taxes. But we can add one more to that list of sure things: hurts. It is inevitable that as we go through life, people will hurt us; and though it might be unintentional, we will hurt people. You know the saying: "Life happens!" It does, and when it happens to you, be willing to forgive.

Sometimes people hurt us by accident, sometimes it is intentional, and sometimes it is out of ignorance. They hurt us by what they do or say. Sometimes the wounds are superficial and heal quickly, while at other times they are deep and the scars remain a lifetime. But mark it down somewhere along life's excursion, people do hurt us!

Don't let your hurt turn into hate, because the effects of hate and bitterness are deadly. They are like acid. They do more damage in the vessel that stores it than the object of the hate.

Harboring hate and bitterness increases your blood pressure. Emotionally, hate and bitterness contribute to depression; spiritually, they hinder worship and prayer; and socially, they make you a sourpuss and unpleasant to be around.

I read of a man named John who as a little boy was sweet with a pleasant personality—a real delight to be around. But by the time he reached retirement age, he had become the community crank. He had a sour personality, full of cynicism and suspicion.

One day when his wife asked him how he wanted his eggs cooked for breakfast, he said, "I want one boiled and one fried." When she brought them to him, he grumbled that she boiled the wrong one.

Have you ever run across someone who was so down on life that they are painful to be around? How did they get this way? That negative spirit is nothing more than an outward reflection of the bottled-up resentment. And it doesn't take very long for some people to get to this stage.

Dr. S.I. McMillen wrote in *None of These Diseases*:

> The moment I start hating a man... or build resentment... I become a slave. I can't enjoy my work anymore because that person even controls my thoughts. My resentments produce too many stress hormones in my body and I become fatigued after only a few hours of work. The work I used to perform now becomes a drudgery... even vacations cease to give me pleasure. The man I resent hounds me wherever I go. I can't escape his grip on my mind.[1]

It is said that the grizzly bear can whip almost any animal in the West. But there is one animal the grizzly will allow to eat with it, even though it resents the intrusion. Do you know what that animal is? The skunk. The grizzly deeply resents the skunk's intrusion, but it is better to coexist than to pay the high price of getting even. The moral of this story is this: Don't retaliate when someone hurts you. All you'll succeed in doing is creating a big stink.

Imagine if we all had the attitude of an eye for an eye and a tooth for a tooth. We would all be blind and toothless.

The apostle Paul wrote this about Alexander, a person who did Paul much harm: "The Lord will repay him for what he has done."

There seems to be an unspoken universal law: hurt people hurt people; healed people heal people.

Forgiveness frees both the wounded and the one who wounds.

Forgiveness frees both the victim and the offender. Forgiveness frees in such a way that lives are transformed, reconstructed, and recreated. Forgiveness is always a miracle, an act of divinity, a moment of sacred manifestation when heaven comes down and glory fills the soul.

When someone hurts you, it can shake your frame, throw off your equilibrium, paralyze your emotions. It seems like you can't shake the divorce, the abuse, the incident, and the feelings of rejection. It can cause you to live in withdrawal—you pull into your shell, build up a wall, resign from life, and refuse to let anybody close to you, not even God, because it hurts so deeply. But God speaks to you when you hurt: "The LORD is close to the brokenhearted and saves those who are crushed in spirit" (Ps. 34:18).

I learned that you have to take the high road with low people. The real question is, do I want to get well, or do I want to get even? Jesus was abused on the cross, with many physical and emotional wounds, but His deepest wounds were His hidden wounds: betrayal, rejection, hate, denial, injustice. Even in the midst of His suffering, He said, "Father, forgive them, for they do not know what they are doing" (Luke 23:34).

Medical doctors and scientists have linked unforgiveness and bitterness with certain diseases, such as arthritis and cancer. Many cases of mental illness are tied to bitter unforgiveness. Maybe you've heard this saying: "Let go and let God." It means let go of your bitterness, let go of your unforgiveness, and let God heal your hurts.

As a young leader I was many times hurt by the things people said and did. Because I liked everybody, I assumed everyone liked me. But I got a reality check early on and realized that there are all kinds of people: some people are mean, ignorant, and downright evil. Then God told me that I would have to grow up quick and get some tough skin if I was going to stay in the ministry.

Ask God to give you tough skin and a soft heart.

In life it's a sure thing that people will hurt us, and sometimes people who are the closest to us hurt us the most. On other occasions someone we don't even know hurts us by passing on rumors or lying about us. One of the biggest tests of life is knowing how to forgive someone who has hurt you, lied about you, spread false rumors about you, and, most important, betrayed you. One thing is for sure: don't get even, because it won't take away your pain. The best thing to do is to pray and ask God to give you a heart to forgive. I know your pain is real and the hurt may still linger, but in order to live you must forgive. You must be have the will to let go and let God. When you are in the prison of your bitterness, forgiveness is the key that sets you free.

Forgiveness adds years to our life.

There was a time I was very bitter toward my third to the oldest brother, Ken. Growing up we had a family business my father had established, which was our only source of income. My father was a good businessman and employed many people in the inner city. When he unexpectedly died, Ken took over the business. He was only twenty at the time. What we did not understand was that he had been using cocaine off and on, which escalated to crack cocaine. Although he was a functioning drug addict running the family business my father left for the family, it was only a matter of time before Ken's addiction caught up with him and he was no longer able to manage the business. So Lindsey's Delivery Service folded. Some of our biggest clients were from two of Houston's most prominent communities, River Oaks and Memorial. Today we could be running a multimillion-dollar company with several locations throughout the country, but because of bad choices by my brother Ken, we lost a golden opportunity as well as our immediate income. This forced Mom back to work after twenty-three years of being a stay-at-home mom. For many years I struggled with releasing Ken from my anger, because his addiction caused so much pain to his family.

I kept thinking about where my family could have been financially if Ken hadn't ruined the business; where my siblings and I could have been in our careers. I kept thinking about the legacy my father wanted to leave, and the business he birthed so that his children, grandchildren, and future generations would always have a place of employment. The more I thought about it, the angrier I became.

But I came to a point where I realized I couldn't change the decisions my brother had made; I could no longer keep holding on to what he did; I could no long keep holding his actions against him. To free him of his actions was really to free myself. I forgave my brother. It was just much healthier for me to let it go and move on. Dr. Martin Luther King Jr. said, "Forgiveness is not an occasional act; it is a permanent attitude."

I must be honest and admit that I still think about how our lives might have been different if we still had the family business. We could have created jobs for many minorities, but I don't dwell on it. I can say that I have moved on, forgiven my brother, and have channeled my energy toward other assignments. As I matured, I realized that if I didn't forgive my brother, I would be worse off than him.

Today my brother is in his fourth year of recovery; he's working every day and serving in ministry. He has a will to become more than his past. I'm so proud of him, and I tell him all the time he is forgiven. Someone once said, "For every sixty seconds you're angry, you lose one minute of happiness."

In his blog, John Maxwell quoted Elbert Hubbard:

> A retentive memory may be a good thing, but the ability to forget is the true token of success. Successful people forget. They know the past is irrevocable. They're running a race. They can't afford to look behind. Their eye is on the finish line. Magnanimous people forget. They're too big to let little things disturb them. They forget easily. If anyone does them wrong, they consider the source and keep cool. It's only the small people who cherish revenge.[2]

What a wakeup call. When I forgave my brother, I let myself off the hook. When someone hurts you deeply, "Play It Down and Pray It Up."

Joseph in the Bible had to forgive his brothers for selling him into prison. Joseph confronted them many years later and said, "What you meant for evil, God meant for good" (Gen. 50:20).

The Will To Be

Sometimes it's helpful to pray "The Serenity Prayer": God grant me the serenity to accept the things I cannot change, the courage to change the things I can and the wisdom to know the difference.

Revealing the hurt and the pain from your past is one of the healthiest decisions you make on your road to healing. As David Seamands said, "When painful memories have not been faced, healed, and integrated into life, they often break through defense and interfere with normal living."

Staying angry at someone who has hurt you is like drinking poison and hoping that your enemy will die. Unforgiveness hurts us more than it does anyone else. Joyce Meyers once said, "Do yourself a favor, forgive!" And George Herbert said, "He who cannot forgive others breaks the bridge over which he himself must travel." One of the main reasons we struggle to accept God's forgiveness is that we cannot forgive ourselves.

Revealing the hurt and the pain from your past is one of the healthiest decisions you make on your road to healing and recovery. Revealing feelings is the beginning to healing.

Mother Teresa quoted Kent M. Keith when she said,

> People are often unreasonable, irrational, and self-centered.
> Forgive them anyway.
> If you are kind, people may accuse you of selfish, ulterior motives.
> Be kind anyway.
> If you are successful, you will win some unfaithful friends and some genuine enemies.
> Succeed anyway.
> If you are honest and sincere people may deceive you.
> Be honest and sincere anyway.
> What you spend years creating, others could destroy overnight.

Create anyway.
If you find serenity and happiness, some may be jealous.
Be happy anyway.
The good you do today, will often be forgotten.
Do good anyway.
Give the best you have, and it will never be enough.
Give your best anyway.
In the final analysis, it is between you and God.
It was never between you and them anyway.

Roberto Assagioli leaves us with something to ponder: "Without forgiveness, life is an endless cycle of resentment." If we are not careful, we begin to resemble the people we resent. Be willing to release all your offenders and get to your place of promise and prosperity.

Takeaway Points

Let go and let God.
To live you must forgive.
If you don't forgive, you'll be worse off than the person you need to forgive.
Play it down and pray it up.

Questions to Reflect On

Can you recall when you needed someone's forgiveness?
How do you act when you need to show forgiveness?
Do you know the difference between forgiveness and reconciliation?
How does unforgiveness hurt us in the long run?

15

The Will to Invest in Others

*Life's most persistent and urgent question is what are you doing
for others?*

—Dr. Martin Luther King Jr.

Loren Eiseley tells the story of "The Star Thrower":

One morning, while a man was walking along the
shore, he looked down the beach and saw a human
figure moving like a dancer. He smiled to himself
at the thought of someone who would dance to the
day, and so he walked faster to catch up. As he got
closer, he noticed that the figure was that of a young
man, and that what he was doing was not dancing
at all. The young man was reaching down to the
shore, picking up small objects, and throwing them
into the ocean. He came closer still and called out,

"Good morning! May I ask what it is that you are doing?"

The young man paused, looked up, and replied "Throwing starfish into the ocean."

"I must ask, then, why are you throwing starfish into the ocean?" asked the somewhat startled wise man.

To this, the young man replied, "The sun is up and the tide is going out. If I don't throw them in, they'll die."

Upon hearing this, the wise man commented, "But, young man, do you not realize that there are miles and miles of beach and there are starfish all along every mile? You can't possibly make a difference!"

At this, the young man bent down, picked up yet another starfish, and threw it into the ocean. As it met the water, he said, "I made a difference for that one." You must be willing to make a difference in the lives of others.[1]

Speaking positive affirmations into one's life can be the lift that people need.

Many people have been thrown to the ground and just need someone to come by and pick them up. When we pick up someone like this, we are making a noticeable difference in their lives.

That's what Janet Habit did for me. I was a struggling high school student, failing and just trying to finish school when one of our Sunday school teachers, who also was a school teacher, decided to take me under her wing. Janet taught night school as well, which I was able to attend to catch up the classes I had already failed in the ninth and tenth grades. She not only taught me in night school and helped me improve my learning skills on the eleventh grade level, she also gave me a ride home the nights she taught me. She mentored me and helped me finish school. She unselfishly reached down and pulled me up by investing her time, skills, and knowledge into my life. I can't imagine where I would be if she had not made that investment into my life at the time I needed encouragement. Ms. Habit not only invested in my life, she invested in the lives of all her students through the many years of teaching. I will always be in debt to her for her wisdom and leadership.

As I prepared for my 2014 graduation at Indiana Wesleyan University, I ordered my cap and gown. I learned that I could order a certificate of appreciation. I ordered two, one for my mom, the late Jewel D. Lindsey, who had passed three-and-a-half months before my graduation, for all her love, leadership, and prayers for the last forty-eight years of my life; and another one for Ms. Janet Habit, for investing in me. I will always be in debt to her for the unselfish contributions and words she deposited into my educational and spiritual life.

Sometimes we simply need to speak encouraging words into the lives of others, because words can be a great investment. John Maxwell said, "Many people go far in life because someone else thought they could."

Words we speak into others are the paintbrush to the canvas of their souls. The question is, what kind of picture am I painting? Every time I speak positive energy into someone's life, I affect them in a positive way. When I see how productive my children are, it's because my wife and I have always spoken positive words of affirmation into their lives.

If the Old Testament prophet Ezekiel could speak life into the dry bones, surely we can speak life into the hearts of those who are cemented in pain, poverty, and problems. We are responsible for helping the down and out, the disconnected, and the disenfranchised. When we lift others, we lift ourselves.

We are our brother's keeper, and we never arrive until everyone else arrives.

Speaking words of faith and affirmation into the lives of others can be one of the greatest investments we ever make. The kids on the playground had it wrong when they said, "Sticks and stones may break my bones but words will never hurt me." That sounds good, but it's not true. The truth is, words hurt and cut deeply, and they oftentimes leave lifetime scars. Your bones may heal in six months, your emotions may take six years. Many parents scar their kids with words; spouses scar their mates with words. On the other hand, many parents speak positive things into their children. Investing in others by speaking positive things over their lives can be a game changer.

In her book *The Power of Positive Prophecy*, Laurie Beth Jones tells a story about a man named Michael:

> I grew up in an alcoholic household where I never heard a positive word. On my way home from school I would always stop in at Jimmy's, the local dry cleaner, because he kept candy on the counter. He got to know me, and told me one afternoon. "Michael, you are a very smart boy. Someday you are going to run a very big business."
>
> I would listen to him in disbelief and return home only to get called a "dog" and knocked around by my dad. But you know... Jimmy the dry cleaner was the only person I can remember believing in me.... Today I run a multimillion-dollar health care organization, just like Jimmy predicted. I guess you could say that a dry cleaner was the prophet in my life.[2]

> *We all can be prophets and prophetess
> who speak into the lives of others who are
> downtrodden, discouraged, and defeated.*

The story of Johnny (Jay) Tyler is another great example of a man who invested his life to help others. I will never forget the day I met Johnny, when he showed up at my office to ask me to officiate at his marriage to his fiancée, Cherri. Johnny wore a big happy smile; he was happy about his new life and freedom. You see, Johnny had made some mistakes in his late teens, which led him to serve time in prison. But now Johnny was starting his life over in church.

I had witnessed progress in him, but then Johnny would slack off. Finally, after a few years of being inconsistent, he finally became one of my best leaders in our church. Everyone loved and respected Johnny because of his love for God and for people. Johnny would help as many people as possible. It came naturally to him. If your car was broken down on the side of the road, he would pull over and assist.

My wife and I would hang out with Johnny and his wife, along with our kids, on Sunday nights at the local bookstore. We would drink coffee, read good books, talk about ministry and life. It was one way we would unwind after a long weekend.

One winter night in January 2003, Jay was leaving work and happened to see a mother and her daughter whose car was broken down on the highway. Johnny pulled over to assist them. While walking back to his vehicle, he was struck and killed by an oncoming car. He invested his life but it cost his own.

I will never forget my phone ringing that night when I received the news of his death. My world was rocked and my life changed forever. I lost one of my best leaders and a great friend. The next day the newspaper called Johnny (Jay) Tyler a "Good Samaritan."

Many of us want to be remembered for what we have done, but not Johnny. He just wanted to invest in other people. He was warned about pulling over and helping strangers, but he said he would always do it. If he could do it all over differently, he wouldn't. He had the will to invest in others. He lost his one life to save two lives. Whether it was coworkers, youth in the church, friends in the community, or a stranded mother and daughter on side of the road, Johnny just wanted to be a help.

His life and legacy will never be forgotten because of his investment in so many lives and his service to humanity and ministry.

According to Karen Bolla, a Johns Hopkins researcher, these are the top five things people most often forget:

1. Names
2. Where something is
3. Telephone numbers
4. Words
5. Faces

One thing you can never forget is a righteous person who invested in others. "A righteous man will be remembered forever" (Ps. 112:6b).

Dr. Martin Luther King Jr. once said, "Everybody can be great . . . because anybody can serve. You don't have to have a college degree to serve. You don't have to make your subject and verb agree to serve. You only need a heart full of grace, a soul generated by love."

When we invest in others, we must be motivated by love.

Hal David was right when he penned the words to the classic song "What the World Needs Now Is Love":

What the world needs now is love sweet love,

It's the only thing that there's just too little of.

Everyone needs love: the rich, the poor, the white, the black, the learned, the unlearned, the fortunate, and the unfortunate. We all need love and we should all share it. Henry Drummond said, "You will find as you look back upon your life that the moments when you have really lived are the moments when you have done things in the spirit of love."

You and I can do various acts of generosity or kindness to invest in others.

- Greet someone with a smile.
- Call someone to see how they are doing.
- Hold the elevator door for a stranger.
- Buy someone lunch.
- Mentor someone.
- Pray for someone.

We can do small acts of kindness that pay big dividends. Research indicates that those who consistently help other people experience less depression, greater calm, fewer pains, and better health. They may even live longer. I'm in the people business: to help people's lives become more fulfilled. People need hope and healing. I use the Bible, prayer, positive affirmations, and encouraging words to help inspire people, to help people get unstuck and reach their God-given potential.

Mother Teresa said, "The world today is hungry not only for bread but hungry for love; hungry to be wanted, to be loved."

No matter how high you go in life, remember to help lift someone else up.

To be great is to be a servant. Find someone to serve, someone to help, and someone to love. If you want to volunteer for an organization, invest in finding the right match. Consider

- volunteering at a school or tutoring program;
- volunteering to clean up a local park;
- working with immigrants;
- making fund-raising calls;
- volunteering as a coach for Little League;
- volunteering at a local hospital or clinic;
- donating food, clothing, or money; or
- working with Habitat for Humanity.

This list could go on and on about how we can invest ourselves: in those who have been struck with a physical disability, the loss of a job, or the death of a spouse or a child. Sometimes the smallest acts of kindness go a long way.

Jesus told us to love the least of society's people. One person like you can change a community, a city, and a country. You must have the will to love, support, and help someone else.

> ## *If we dare to care for others, we can change the world one person at a time.*

A Franciscan Benediction goes like this:

> May God bless you with tears to shed for those who suffer from pain, rejection, starvation, and war, so that you may reach out your hand to comfort them and to turn their pain into joy. And may God bless you with enough foolishness to believe that you can make a difference in this world, so that you can do what others claim cannot be done.

What a powerful prayer that God would keep each of us discomforted to help those who need comfort. You can be one person who can make a huge difference in the world. You may tell yourself that you are just one person, but you might be the one person to save some company, some organization, some community, or some child. Your presence can be a gift to the world. Let me ask you a question: Will you help someone today, or will you turn away?

Johnny Tyler lived in such a way that his living was not in vain. He didn't live a long life, but his was a well-lived life for most of his twenty-eight years.

It takes only one person to make a difference: you!

It's not the duration of your life, it's the donation of your life that counts.

Takeaway Points

When we lift others, we lift ourselves.
We all need love, and we should all share it.
We can do small acts of kindness that can pay big dividends.
It takes only one person to make a difference: you!

Questions to Reflect On

What investments will you make in the lives of others?
What are some ways you can speak positive affirmations into the lives of others?
How will you inspire others to become more than what they are?
Who are you currently mentoring?

16

The Will to Pray

Prayer is a miracle waiting to happen.

—Unknown

Prayer is one of the most powerful and most neglected weapons in the world.

I can't imagine life without prayer. Without prayer I would have no sense of direction and guidance. Prayer helps us depend on God's leading in our lives. I love Josh Groban's lyrics from the song, "The Prayer." I have played it many times before making big decisions. I've listened to it during times in my life when I wasn't sure what the next family move or ministry move would be. The first two verses ask the Lord to "be our eyes . . . help us be wise . . . guide us with Your grace."

One thing I know is that prayer is one of the best ways to deal with the challenges of life. Prayer is the solution to the problems of life.

Sometimes you can't see your way until you pray your way.

Prayer is the most powerful weapon we have to deal with life. I can tell countless stories of how prayer opened doors for my life and allowed me to experience the miracles of God.

In 2003, when my wife, Shawn, was diagnosed with leukemia at the age of thirty-one, I immediately began to pray. We had some prayer gatherings, one prayer vigil at our church and another with close family and friends at our home the night before she was to be admitted in M. D. Anderson Cancer Center in Houston's Medical Center. We prayed and prayed and then prayed some more. The result was that God healed my wife. It was still a tough process she had to experience, losing her hair twice and going through eight rounds of chemo, but we prayed each step of the way, and God helped us through one of the toughest seasons of our life.

Each of us possesses the will to pray. We can worry or pray. We can complain or pray. We can become defeated or pray. I have chosen to make prayer a daily part of my life. Each day we are faced with new challenges and circumstances, and that's why we should always pray.

The Word of God tells us that we should always pray and not faint. I see many people giving up on their hopes and dreams. It easy to give up and to quit in life, but it takes a person with a will, with a burning determination, to pray one more time.

Sometimes you have to pray a Jehoshaphat prayer. He was a good king, a faithful king, and a godly king. Yet this did not exempt Jehoshaphat from the threat of trouble. A vast army stood against Jehoshaphat; three nations conspired to work together to utterly destroy Judah. And what was Jehoshaphat's response?

Jehoshaphat prayed one of the most powerful prayers of all time. "O our God, won't you stop them? We are powerless against this mighty army that is about to attack us. We do not know what to do, but we are looking to you for help" (2 Chron. 20:12 NLT).

They key to dealing with life's problems is always to look to God. Prayer is talking to God and Him talking back to you.

Stevie Wonder sang "Have a Talk with God": "Every problem has an answer . . . when you feel your life's too hard . . . have a talk with God."

You can make it through life when you talk and walk with God. I remember having to talk and cry to Him on many occasions. When my father was dying from a second massive stroke when I was seventeen, I cried and talked to God as I stood outside of St. Luke's hospital in Houston's Medical Center District on a hot summer night in July 1983. When the church I planted struggled to grow in the early '90s, I cried and talked to God. When Mom was sick in 2011 and 2012 and had to be hospitalized, I cried and talked to God. When I received a devastating phone call on January 1, 2014, telling me that my mother had just died unexpectedly, I cried and talked to God. When one of my most dedicated church members was killed in a tragic accident in 2003, I cried and talked to God.

Prayer has always been a healthy way for me to release pain. Through prayer I am able to release stress, hurt, and pain that could eventually cause illness in my body. So many people medicate their pain through drug use, alcohol, sex, gambling, and overeating. If only they would look up and talk to God through prayer, they would discover that God is just a prayer away. Martin Luther said, "The less I pray, the harder it gets;

the more I pray the better it goes." That's been my story, and I know that prayer is an equal-opportunity factor. God will not only listen to your prayers, He will answer your prayers. But you must be willing to continue in prayer.

When we continue in prayer, we show God how serious we are about what we are praying for.

F. B. Meyer once said, "The great tragedy of life is not unanswered prayer, but unoffered prayer." We stop praying too soon, that's why this chapter is called "The Will to Pray." Pray until you get an answer. Prayer is never a waste of time, and no praying is ever in vain. Bill Hybels said that when we work, we work, but when we pray, God works. Let God work for you while you work in prayer.

Abraham Lincoln said, "I have been driven many times upon my knees by the overwhelming conviction that I had nowhere else to go. My own wisdom and that of all about me is insufficient for that day." Continuing in prayer can be the factor that gets you to the next level of living and becoming more than what you are.

Prayer is a miracle waiting to happen.

I dare you to pray in faith. Don't just pray; pray with faith. Pray believing and expecting. If prayer is the key, trust me, faith will unlock the door. I still believe that just a little talk with Jesus makes everything all right. Don't worry, just pray, and if you pray as much as you worry, you will have much less to worry about.

Takeaway Points

Prayer helps us depend on God's leading in our lives.
Each of us possesses the will to pray.
Let God work for you, while you work in prayer.
Don't just pray; pray with faith.

Questions to Reflect On

Why do people not take advantage of the power of prayer?
What does continuing in prayer say to God?
In what ways has God answered your prayers?
How does linking prayer and faith make a difference?

17

The Will to Leave a Legacy

Our days are numbered. One of the primary goals in our lives should be to prepare for our last day. The legacy we leave is not just in our possessions, but in the quality of our lives. What preparations should we be making now? The greatest waste in all of our earth, which cannot be recycled or reclaimed, is our waste of the time that God has given us each day.

—Billy Graham

Legacy is a strong word that we often take for granted. It has so much more meaning to me since Mom's unexpected death on January 1, 2014. Now I have also begun to think about my own legacy.

Saint Augustine said, "Asking yourself the question of your own legacy—What do I wish to be remembered for?—is the beginning of adulthood." Wow!

On January 11, 2014, we celebrated the life, love, leadership, and legacy of my mother, Mrs. Jewel Delores Lindsey. That little five-foot-six lady from Franklin, Texas, gave life all she had and with dignity and grace. Benjamin Franklin said, "Most men die at age twenty-five but are not buried until age seventy." Not Mrs. Jewel Lindsey. She died at age seventy-five, and she was buried at age seventy-five. I can't give you the totality of her life in one chapter, for that would not be sufficient, but I will give you the CliffsNotes of her life.

I could talk about her life because it was purposeful; I could talk about her leadership because it was resilient; I could talk about her personality because it was magnetic; but I want to talk about her love, which was her legacy.

The legacy of love and wisdom she left will carry my family and future generations for centuries to come. I could brag on her because of her tenacious living, strong work ethic, and homemade cooking. She was a great wife and a friend to many. As one of her biggest fans, I could go on talking about how she paid off her house and life insurance as a widow in her late sixties. I can praise her because of her spiritual accuracy, her love for God, and her daily devotion in prayer and in the Word.

She was more than just a mother; she was a teacher, leader, and coach. I saw her go from a good mother to a great mother to a legendary mother.

She taught us with her words, wisdom, and walk. "She speaks with wisdom, and faithful instruction is on her tongue" (Prov. 31:26).

The old saying is true: "Some things are not taught, but caught." Our home was a university, church, and seminary. It was a place of learning, growing, discipline, and development. She shared her many insights that have guided our family for over half a century. She had a fun, upbeat personality, full of life and laughter. She was intelligent, polite, and honest. You wanted to visit Mom often, and the welcome mat was always on the front porch.

Mom and I shared the same birthday, a winter Friday on January 28, separated by twenty-eight years. A strong influence in my life, she helped to shape me into the person I am. I learned a lot from her words, wisdom, and walk. She was my model, motivator, and mentor.

Mother Jewel Lindsey was a precious jewel, a precious gem. Some people are silver, and some people are gold, but Jewel Lindsey was platinum. When I grow up, I want to be just like Jewel Lindsey. In the words of Abraham Lincoln, "All that I am or ever hope to be, I owe to my angel mother."

All the love she showed my family was part of her legacy. Mother never attended college, she never earned a six-figure income, she never wrote a book, but she did something greater: she loved and left an inheritance of love. My family is richer because of it, her church is richer because of it, this world is richer because of it. She loved all people, the lovely and the unlovely. Rudy Rasmus wrote in his excellent book *Touch: Pressing Against the Wounds of a Broken World*, "I believe God has put it in the hearts of all true believers to love the unlovely."

Mom knew how to love, how to care, and how to support others. She was always checking on others, calling others on the phone, mailing encouraging cards. They would often call her Mrs. Hallmark. Her life was bigger than herself because she made it about others. She didn't pretend to love, she authentically loved. Dr. Martin Luther King Jr. said, "Life's most urgent and persistent question is, what are we doing for others?" My mom was always doing something for others. She made love a priority. Since her passing, many of her friends express to me how much they miss her love.

Rick Warren, author of the *The Purpose Driven Life,* wrote: "Love will last forever. . . . Love leaves a legacy. How you treat people, not your wealth or accomplishments, is the most enduring impact you can leave on earth."[1]

Mother Teresa said, "The greatest science in the world, in heaven and on earth, is love." My mother will be remembered for her love. I want to learn to love like her, to love like Jesus modeled for us to love. Even when sickness invaded her body the last two years of her life, she was still willing to live and to love. She began to love even harder and deeper. Never complaining but always loving. She had the will to love even in the midst of pain and discomfort. She never allowed her pain to cause her to have mood swings; she was always the same loving Jewel Lindsey. Although she's not here physically, but home with Jesus, her spirit of love and the impact she made on so many lives will always be felt and remembered.

How do you want to be remembered? What will they say about you once you're gone? What mark will you leave behind? What dent will you leave in the universe? What will be said at your funeral? What will be written on your headstone? What will your epitaph say? How will you be commemorated? What will they say during your eulogy? These are questions only you can answer. Travis Smiley said, "The choices we make about the lives we live determine the kinds of legacies we leave."

The way we live each day we are writing out our eulogies and legacies.

In the end, your legacy won't be about what university you attended, what degrees you earned, what company you worked for, what sorority or fraternity you belonged to; it won't be about your economic status, where you lived, or what you drove; it will be about who you loved, who you supported, and who you cared for. The old saying is true, "People don't care how much we know until they first know how much we care."

This is your time to write your legacy by loving God and others more deeply and consistently. Love is a choice, not an emotional feeling. Love is something we exercise, regardless of how we feel. Remember, love is a verb. It makes you act, and the more you love, you will begin to see your potential to love grow even stronger. This is what makes your legacy great. Shannon L. Alder said, "Carve your name on hearts, not tombstones."

When you die, what will they say about you? Someone once said, "Live in such a way that when the minister preaches your eulogy, he will be telling all the truth." It is every human's utmost desire to bequeath a mark or impression on the world.

Each and every day gives us numerous opportunities to make a small difference by showing small or large acts of kindness.

Your legacy starts with you, right now. My mother's passing was truly unexpected. We were shocked, hurt, and discombobulated. Randy Alcorn said, "The time of our death is unknown. The way of our death is unpredictable. The fact of our death is inescapable." Quick question, what are the odds you will die someday? The odds are in your favor. You have a 100 percent chance of dying someday. We have an appointment with death and we won't be late in arriving.

A legacy is not only about producing results or record-breaking achievements; a legacy is about serving others. A legacy is a lifetime of work and transpires every day.

> *Are we leaving the world a better place than how we found it? Jewel Delores Lindsey left this world a much better place. She is a legacy leaver. This world needs more people like Jewel Lindsey.*

It's unhealthy to live in denial of death. The older you get the more you need to think about death and the legacy you will leave behind. My mother not only lived, she outlived her life. She had the will to leave a legacy, and she did. Benjamin Franklin said, "If you would not be forgotten as soon as you are dead, either write something worth reading or do something worth writing." Jewel Delores Lindsey lived in such a way that her legacy is truly worth writing.

What about your legacy?

Remember today is the first day of the best of your life. Make your life count and make your legacy epic!

Takeaway Points

The way we live each day we are writing out our eulogy and legacy.

Love is something we exercise, regardless of how we feel.

We have an appointment with death.

Your legacy starts with you, right now.

Questions to Reflect On

Are you doing things that are significant and enduring?

What stories will others tell about you in the future?

What will they learn from your legacy?

In what ways are you making a difference?

Notes

Chapter 1
1. Kirbyjon H. Caldwell, *The Gospel of Good Success: A Road Map to Spiritual, Emotional and Financial Wholeness* (Fireside, 1999), 16.

Chapter 2
1. Ira Flatow, *They All Laughed . . . From Light Bulbs to Lasers* (New York: HarperCollins, 1992).
2. Phinehas Kinuthia, *From Dreaming to Belonging* (2013).

Chapter 4
1. Vincent Fortanasce, MD, *The Anti-Alzheimer's Prescription: The Science-Proven Plan to Start at Any Age* (New York: Gotham books, 2008), 54.
2. Samuel DuBois Cook, "The Wisdom *de Profundis* of Benjamin E. Mays, Black Colleges, and the Good Life," *Quarterly Review: A Journal of Theological Resources of*

Ministry, Vol. 15, No. 2 (Summer 1995), 129, http://www.quarterlyreview.org/pdfs/VOL15NO2SUMMER1995.pdf.

3. Chuck Swindoll, Goodreads, http://www.goodreads.com/quotes/267482-the-longer-i-live-the-more-i-realize-the-impact.

Chapter 5

1. Mark H. McCormack, *What They Don't Teach You in Harvard Business School: Notes from a Street-Smart Executive*, (New York: Bantam Books, 1986).
2. Brian Tracy, *Goals! How to Get Everything You Want—Faster Than You Ever Thought Possible* (San Francisco: Berrett-Koehler Publishers, Inc. 2010), 59.
3. James C. Collins and Jerry I. Porras, "Building Your Company's Vision," *Harvard Business Review* (September–October 1996), 73.
4. Og Mandino, *The Greatest Secret in the World* (New York: Random House Publishing Group, 1997), 38.

Chapter 6

1. David A. Seamands and Beth Funk, *Healing for Damaged Emotions Workbook* (Colorado Springs, CO: David C. Cook, 2004), 81.
2. Charles C. Finn, "Please Hear What I'm Not Saying," in *Please Hear What I'm Not Saying* (1966). http://www.poetrybycharlescfinn.com/pleasehear.html.

Chapter 7

1. Lynn Woodard, "Why Me?" *Learning from Life*, May 1, 2010, http://www.learningfromlynn.com/2010/05/why-me.html.

Chapter 8

1. Dan Zadra, *Where Will You Be Five Years From Today?* (Seattle, WA: Compendium, Inc., 2009), 30.

Chapter 9

1. Rory Vaden, *Take the Stairs: 7 Steps to Achieving True Success* (Penguin Group, 2012), Introduction.
2. Richard Leider and Steven Buchholz, "The Rustout Syndrome," *Training & Development* Vol. 49, no. 3 (March 1995), 7.

Chapter 10

1. Dr. Ron Brown, *The Courageous Life* (Dream Time Publishing, 2009), 28.
2. *Ibid.*, 170–171.

Chapter 11

1. T.D. Jakes, *Maximize the Moment: God's Action Plan for Your Life* (New York: Berkley Publishing Group; Putnam Copying,1999), 164–165.
2. "Bouncing Back Big Time: Top Ten Comebacks," *Sports Illustrated*, November 2001, http://sportsillustrated.cnn.com/vault/article/magazine/MAG1024225/index.htm.

Chapter 12

1. Jim Burns, *The Purity Code: God's Plan for Sex and Your Body* (Bloomington, MN: Bethany House, 2008), 63.

Chapter 13

1. Howard R. Lewis and Martha E. Lewis, "Child's Death in London Laid to Fear of Dentist," *Psychosomatics* (New York: Viking Press, 1975), 27.

2. Bruce Wilkinson, David Kopp, and Heather Kopp, *The Dream Giver* (Colorado Springs, CO: Multnomah Books, 2003), 86.
3. Paul Wilson Jr., *Dream Big in 3D: How to Pursue a Bold, Innovative, God-Inspired Life!* (ParaMind Publications, 2009), 95.
4. *Underdog,*Wikipedia, http://en.wikipedia.org/wiki/Underdog_(TV_series).

Chapter 14
1. Ray Burwick, "Anger 12: Bitterness," *Gain Through Loss*, July 18, 2008, http://gainthroughloss.blogspot.com/2008_07_01_archive.html.
2. John Maxwell, "Burning Bridges," *The John Maxwell Co.*, November 16, 2012, http://www.johnmaxwell.com/blog/burning-bridges.

Chapter 15
1. Loren Eiseley, "The Star Thrower," *The Unexpected Universe* (Orlando, FL: Harcourt Brace & Co., 1969).
2. Laurie Beth Jones, *The Power of Positive Prophecy: Finding the Hidden Potential in Everyday Life* (1999).

Chapter 17
1. Rick Warren, *The Purpose Driven Life* (Grand Rapids, MI: Zondervan, 2002), 127.

About the Author

A native Houstonian, William J. Lindsey is the founding pastor of Above & Beyond Fellowship, a thirteen-acre campus in Spring, Texas, a suburb of Houston. William and his wife, Shawn, began the ministry in 1993, and it has now grown into more than 1,400 members.

A student of great leaders, William received his Bachelor's Degree in Leadership from the College of Biblical Studies in 2003, attended Regent University's Master's program in Organizational Leadership, and received his Master's Degree in Leadership from Indiana Wesleyan University in 2014. William is a currently pursuing a Doctorate of Ministry degree with a specialization in Leadership at Laurel University "High Point, NC".

Certified as a Life Coach and a Church Consultant, William serves at Senior Consultant for Coach Me to Lead, a leadership network for individuals, leaders, and churches. William believes that life should be lived above mediocrity. William has appeared on KHCB, KMJQ FM, and KTSU FM radio stations.

William is also the author of *Unstuck 101: How to Double Clutch Your Life* and *Becoming More: A Greater Degree of You.* Released in 2015.

William blogs at www.willjlindsey.com
William Tweets at www.twitter.com/willjlindsey

For more information about William J. Lindsey and the services he offers, visit www.willjlindsey.com

UNSTUCK 101

ARE YOU STUCK IN A RUT?
ARE YOU STUCK IN MEDIOCRITY?
ARE YOU STUCK IN APATHY?

I used to be stuck so I can relate to how you feel. Most people just like myself at one point in life occasionally get stuck in a rut. Whether it's emotional, physical, spiritual, or financial, stagnation in life can ruin motivation, drain your momentum, and lead to feelings of emptiness.

The good news is you can get unstuck, and the best news is you can stay unstuck.

Don't settle for the status quo; prepare to double clutch into a new gear and life of intentional living. This book will propel you like a rocket towards new heights and higher dimensions.

"To get unstuck you will have to do a few things really well 1,000 times. If you practice these time-tested principles, I guarantee

they will help you get your life unstuck, out of park, and shifted into another gear of daring excitement and endless propensity. You are no exception! I encourage you to subscribe to these prescriptions and practice them weekly and you will begin to see a much more positive and productive you. Stay with the process and you will eventually see the progress."

—William J. Lindsey, Author

BECOMING MORE

A GREATER DEGREE OF YOU

Becoming More deconstructs and debunks old and defeated thinking patterns that have kept us overwhelmed. This book offers unique and inspiring principles that will help you rise above the chaos and curve to become all that God has destined you to become.

- Embrace Change
- Become Self-Motivated
- Move from Surviving to Thriving
- Use Your God-given Creativity
- Create a Sense of Urgency

"This inspiring work demonstrates how by making revolutionary changes that are absolutely vital, you will position yourself to leap from surviving to thriving. Now is the time for you to create a sense of urgency for your life, career, and future. Make

your life more epic and reach a greater degree of your God-given potential."

—William J. Lindsey, Author

**What if you were given the choice to
become more or stay the same?**

What would you choose?

"How to Write Your First Book."

*"There is no greater agony than bearing
an untold story inside you."*
—Maya Angelou

Don't put off another day on the book that's been stirring your soul. It's time to take your book from your head and put it into the hands of your readers. Don't procrastinate on writing what could very well be a *New York Times* best seller. Who knows? This seminar will show you the nuts and bolts of writing your first book. Here's what you will learn:

- How to Write a Book
- How to Self-Publish
- How to Market Your Book
- How to Build a Platform
- How to Get Endorsers
- How to Earn Multiple Streams of Revenue
- How to Use Social Media
- How to Turn Your Book into a Business
- How to Increase Your Influence and Build Your Tribe
- How to Find a Graphic Designer and Editor

- How to get Your Book on Amazon and Audible
- How to Podcast

With practicality and experience, William will
show you the proven strategies that have worked
for him and other successful authors. Learn
how to write, publish and sell your books.

Michael Hyatt says, *"Nothing gains credentials like writing
a book. Not even a PhD."* Take advantage of this seminar
and finally become the author you were destined to be.

Note: This seminar is for self-publishing,
and not traditional publishers.
For more information, please visit www.willjlindsey.com